BUT CHRIST DID RISE

But Christ Did Rise!

and other Sermons on Lenten Gospels

Lent, 1944

Edited by

PAUL ZELLER STRODACH

THE MUHLENBERG PRESS

PHILADELPHIA : PENNSYLVANIA

Made in the United States of America

Contents

SEPTUAGESIMA

The Great Decision

Robert Harris Gearhart, Jr.

SEPTUAGESIMA

NOW it came to pass, as they went, that he entered into a certain village: and a certain woman, named Martha, received him into her house. And she had a sister called Mary, which also sat at Jesus' feet, and heard his word.

But Martha was cumbered about much serving, and came to him and said, "Lord, dost thou not care that my sister hath left me to serve alone? Bid her therefore that she help me."

And Jesus answered and said unto her, "Martha, Martha, thou art careful and troubled about many things: but one thing is needful: and Mary hath chosen that good part, which shall not be taken away from her." —*Luke 10: 38-42*

The Great Decision

DECISIONS do not happen, they are made.

A number of years ago while motoring in the White Mountains we came upon a road that was being rebuilt. Posted at the side of the highway was the significant sign, "Choose your rut carefully, you will be in it a long time." Accompanying this warning was no suggestion of which rut or why it should be chosen and, although some of us fretted then, most of us were able to smile about it later, for we were in it for a very long time.

Life usually is like that. The choice that changes our entire life, which is made in a moment and seemingly with little or no thought, actually rests upon a foundation that has been long years in building. Decisions have their bases in long years of a developing experience in which chance plays but a small part and which in reality depend on ingrained attitudes and long cultivated preferences. Yesterday, today, and doubtless for many days to come, this is the simple story of life.

One does not read far in the gospel story before he begins to realize how this matter of decisions colors much of it. For one thing no matter where he reads he quickly becomes conscious that he is not often alone with the Master. Everywhere

He went, the people were there. They may not be specifically mentioned in some paragraph but one feels their restlessness, their rudeness, their impatience. They were captious, covetous, careless crowds. They asked catch questions. They constantly wanted new signs and wonders. They quickly became dissatisfied and wandered off to hear or see some new thing. So when we read this story of Mary and Martha (from which the text is taken), and see that Mary had seated herself at the Lord's feet and was listening to His teaching, it does not take any great leap of the imagination to see a considerable body of men and women gathered about the doorway of that Bethany home who likewise listened to His words.

If Jesus were not who He is, it would not be surprising if He had become impatient with those importunate but ineffective people. They were as sheep that had no shepherd, bleating of their needs to sundry and all, yet never realizing that they did not have within them even a knowledge of the shepherd principle.

How many times committees, councils, and commissions have convened, considering the moral and religious needs of some group, and when those requirements have been explored have recommended as a remedy a party, a picnic, or a play? Time-serving devices to distract attention from the very condition which it was their duty to remedy.

Some years ago painstaking historians discovered literally thousands of old yellow manuscripts hidden away in the huge Escorial Palace that once had been the retreat of Philip II of Spain. Some were dispatches from generals pleading for immediate reinforcements. Others were messages from governors imploring instant help. Yet others had come from judges or councilors begging for speedy decisions in weighty matters of state. All of them were endorsed in the crooked, formless writing of the king with the words, "Delay" or "Postpone." Philip was a petty tyrant. He had one man-servant whipped for wasting cord, and another beheaded for eating meat on Friday when no other food was to be had. He cursed and imprisoned men who did not behave as he did and promoted the morally unclean and rewarded murderers. He never was known to make a decision when it could be avoided. He had neither the mental equipment nor the moral courage that makes deciding possible, and when he died the glory, wealth and power that was Spain had totally disappeared.

A wise old pagan once said, "There is no mark for those who miss."

Where the minds of men and women find interest only in petty things, the great and the worthwhile things of life do not exist.

Centuries ago an enterprising family of landscape architects in Japan engaged in the unusual profession of making great things small. After many generations of painstaking labor they succeeded in so dwarfing oak and pine trees that they readily could be cultivated in a tea cup. The secret of their success lay in cutting off the strong central taproot that drives down into the earth.

Jesus probably had just this sort of thing in mind when in the Parable of the Four Kinds of Soil, He spoke of the grain that fell on shallow ground, that sprang up quickly, and then just as quickly withered away. No, the Master did not become impatient with people; He knew them too well. He knew that a great decision could not be made by men and women who had neither rootage nor soil that would make such choice possible.

But while Mary and the crowd listened to Jesus in the dooryard Martha was at work in the house; busy Martha. Hers was no easy task. Jewish dietary laws did not simplify kitchen technique. The sudden arrival of a dozen or more dinner guests would disrupt many a home and when she thought of her sister quietly sitting listening while Jesus taught and she worked, her irritation overflowed in outspoken protest.

How often and how sincerely we sympathize with her. How often we have *felt,* if we did not say or even think it, that the Master was a little unkind, or that He did not fully understand when He mildly rebuked her.

The difficulty was that Martha, like most other people, could not see the forest for the trees. She was so much interested in living that she was not aware of life. Bread for dinner was more important than the Bread that was come down from heaven.

She was made of different stuff than was the crowd at the doorway. She made her decisions and doubtless believed them wisely made. It *was* important that they should eat good, well-prepared food, but was that *the* important thing? It was not every day that Jesus would sit on her threshold teaching. However delicious her dinner it would soon be forgotten and Mary would have much to remember.

Four hundred years ago in the days of Henry VIII of England, Cardinal Wolsey, by bribery, intrigue, and duplicity, sought to promote the monarch's fortunes. Then abandoned and practically alone, on his deathbed he exclaimed, "Had I but served God with half the zeal that I have served my king, in my old age He would not have left me desolate."

Martha's difficulty was not that she lacked a deep, strong taproot to her life, but it was the soil into which that root had grown. She had not listened enough to know what was the really important thing in life. She was anxious and worried about the very things Jesus warned people against when He said, "Be not anxious about what you shall eat or what you shall drink or what you shall wear."

This Bethany home was one of the places where spontaneous affection flowed out to meet the Master and Martha doubtless would have been deeply grieved if anyone had called into question the quality or sincerity of her love, but her fretfulness betrayed her. Sheep grazing in a pasture call forth exclamations of delight, but how seldom we stop to think that few sheep ever raise their eyes above the level of the grass that they nibble. "How much more is a man than a sheep."

For her, Martha's concern was a perfectly normal anxiety. She, like many other deeply religious people of her own or other days, had developed, or had had developed for her, many rules by which to live. Life was a measure to be filled and not a goblet to be drained. It was the score and not the game that was important. If she had heard Jesus say, "I am come that you may have life and may have it more abundantly," she would have been puzzled for there is no rule book for abundant living.

Jesus was not unkind; He did understand, and with kindliness and sympathy no small part of His teaching and life was given to teaching the better way. He said it in so many ways, "Seek ye first the Kingdom of Heaven and all of these things will be added unto you"; "The one built his house upon the sand"; "Where your treasure is there will your heart be also."

At first glance it is a simple easy matter, but actually it is not so. It was new and strange teaching in Jewry in Mary's day, and it is a new thing to many even in this far distant day. We like she must sit and listen, in spite of life, or maybe because of it; although the crowds may jostle or possibly because they do. Notwithstanding the concern of others over nonessentials or perhaps because of their anxiety, if ours is to be the great, the abiding decision, we must quietly take our places by Mary's side and listen to His teaching. It is hard to realize that, "a man's life does not consist in the abundance of the things that he possesses."

A young ruler, whom Luke characterizes as the richest possible man, who had kept all of the commandments from his youth up, was startled and puzzled when Jesus told him that he would find the way into the Kingdom by giving all of his possessions away and by coming and following Him.

The young Roman patrician Marcellus, whom Lloyd Douglass makes the hero of the stirring novel, "The Robe," was no different from the other men of his day. His experience was a long and painfully bought one, and his decision to follow the Galilean was neither easily nor speedily made. When the emperor demanded that, "he give up this foolish obsession about Jesus or Diana your sweetheart will be married to Prince Gaius," it was not as though he had called for a surrender of either wealth or position. It was not for nothing that for weary months he had plodded the dusty miles in Palestine. He had built a real understanding of what Jesus meant when He said, "He that loves father or mother more than me is not worthy of me."

It is just this that the world of men in this day, as every other day, has not learned. In His model for prayer Jesus put as the second petition, "Thy kingdom come." Has that Kingdom come as yet? Well, why not?

Jesus did not refuse to recognize the place and importance of the necessities of life. The very next petition of that prayer pattern has to do with food, but you cannot have freedom from want until the greater necessity has been met, until the great decision has been made.

Jesus did not close His eyes to the depth of joy that grows out of the privilege of human love and companionship. Did He not make provision for His mother's comfort even while He hanged on the Cross; and did He not say, "How can a man love God whom he hath not seen, if he hate his brother whom he hath seen"? Yet the first and the great commandment was, "Thou shalt love the Lord thy God."

This is no medieval mysticism that would lead men into monastic retreat away from an evil world. This is no modern psychological escape mechanism that gets rid of a nasty situation by ignoring it. This is squarely coming to grips with a summation of the cause of every curse of this present-day world and deciding that that which is first shall be first in my life.

With all of our traditions behind and around us, with all of the false values that have been put on rules, things, and the like, it is a fearsome, and many would say, a foolhardy thing to do.

It was a rainy morning twenty-five years ago that I walked with fear and trembling toward an airfield in France. The raindrops that had fallen on the shattered rubbish heaps that once had been homes trickled muddily beside the road. In the not too far distance some guns roared while others chattered. Several comrades denounced my adventure as folly, for that day I was going to fly. Why should I risk my life up there when I was so safe down here? Maybe I was a fool, but I had decided to go; and, after all, was I so safe "down here"? My pilot smiled reassuringly as he strapped me in saying, "Trust me." Then for better or for worse we were off. Rain pelted us, flying metallic hate pursued us—but up—up into the clouds we went. A fork of lightning surprised us, the speedy gale of our own making tore at us, and even the thunder went unheard. In a flash we hurtled out of the mist that clouded our way and that blanketed all that was below. And there under a sky that never had been more blue, in a sun that had never been more cheering, my pilot, God and I were alone together—my pilot was trustworthy.

SEXAGESIMA

The Lord and Giver of Life

Russell D. Snyder

SEXAGESIMA

THEN Martha, as soon as she heard that Jesus was coming, went and met him: but Mary sat still in the house. Then said Martha unto Jesus, "Lord, if thou hadst been here, my brother had not died. But I know, that even now, whatsoever thou wilt ask of God, God will give it thee."

Jesus said unto her, "Thy brother shall rise again."

Martha saith unto him, "I know that he shall rise again in the resurrection at the last day."

Jesus said unto her, "I am the resurrection, and the life: he that believeth in me, though he were dead, yet shall he live: and whosoever liveth and believeth in me shall never die. Believest thou this?"

She saith unto him, "Yea, Lord: I believe that thou art the Christ, the Son of God, which should come into the world."

—*John 11: 20-27*

The Lord and Giver of Life

OUR text is the second act in the drama of the raising of Lazarus,—St. John's report of our Lord's colloquy with Martha as they walked toward the house of mourning. In this memorable colloquy the Lord of Life speaks to our souls about eternal life, its source, and its character.

Shrewd observers have pointed out that every living organism carries within itself a suppressed desire for death. This paradox can be understood only in the light of the fact that every living organism, from the amoeba upward, is involved in the age-old struggle between life and death. The warfare between these two implacable enemies is the story of the life of man. That it is raging on every front is clear from the use which the Evangelist makes of this narrative. Read it again and you will find that the raising of Lazarus became the occasion for a sharpening of the opposition to Jesus. St. John is trying to show how the Lord of Life had to do battle with death in all its forms, spiritual death as well as physical death.

I

The first thought which this portion of the narrative suggests to our minds is that in this area too the Lord of Life is *our Friend and Teacher.* Wondrously intimate and tender were the ties that bound Him to the household at Bethany. We read that He "loved Martha, and her sister, and Lazarus." When Lazarus was taken ill, the two sisters immediately sent for their Friend. Intent upon demonstrating to His followers that, no matter what might happen to the body of one of His friends, He was still the Lord of Life, He delayed His going. Meanwhile, Lazarus died. Then Jesus set out for Bethany to minister to His friends. His loyalty to them comes to us as a reminder that He is not only the Friend of publicans and sinners, He is also the Friend of the Marys and Marthas among us. He is both willing and able to help all who turn to Him for help.

It should be carefully noted, however, that Mary and Martha continued to put their trust in Him in spite of the strain which had just been put upon their friendship for Him. "Lord, if thou hadst been here, my brother had not died." When death threatens to rob us of a loved one, and we summon a physician, especially a physician who is also an intimate friend, we expect immediate action. These women, too, expected immediate action. Instead of immediate action, they got inexplicable delay. Yet they continued to trust Him!

That is the gallantry of soul from which all true faith springs. It is not faith to believe when reason and all the evidences of the senses support faith; faith is to believe and press on when all appearances are against faith. It has been said that a friend is one who understands our silences. Mary and Martha understood our Lord's silence on this occasion, His failure to act in time to save their brother from death.

If we would enter into the riches of His friendship for us, we too must be prepared to understand His silences. We must be prepared to trust Him as a Friend who always has our best interests at heart and would therefore rather hurt us than spoil us; a Friend who, even when He seems to be failing us in a crisis, is but contriving richer and more spacious blessings for us and preparing us for fellowship with Himself. When death comes into our homes, and a loved one is taken from us, we must be prepared to trust Him as one who always knows what is best, best for those whom He takes from us, and best for us who survive.

But we must also be prepared to profit by His Teachings. The Lord of Life is also our Teacher, a Teacher of amazing aptitude and skill, a Teacher who can use our grey days and our bitter moments in order to work out in our lives, or in the lives of others, some holy, beneficent purpose. That is brought out most impressively in this colloquy on the road to Bethany. "Thy brother shall rise again," He said to Martha. Believing that He was referring to the general resurrection, an article of faith which she shared with most of her countrymen, Martha replied, "I know that he shall rise again in the resurrection at the last day." She was trying to draw what comfort she could from the prospect of a general resurrection at the end of the age. Jesus did not say anything to disturb her in this hope. He tacitly put the seal of His divine approval upon it. At the same time He saw that it was affording her meager comfort in her hour of desolation. She was obviously suffering from what Scott has called "the sickening pang of hope deferred." He saw, moreover, that she had missed one of the cardinal lessons of His gospel, namely, that by the grace of God sin and death can be vanquished in this life. That is the only faith that will meet our needs in the tensions and sorrows of the present, when we are fighting for our very lives against sin and death in our own members. In the nature of the case life cannot win unless it wins here and now; it cannot wait until death has had its inning.

II

This brings us to the second thought. The Christ who is revealed to us in this colloquy is *our Life in this world.* "I am the resurrection and the life," He says; "he that believeth in me, though he were dead, yet shall he live."

"I am the resurrection and the life!" This is the most remarkable of that remarkable sequence of "I am" utterances in the Fourth Gospel. Are we hungering after the Bread of Life? "I am the bread of life," says Jesus. Are we thirsting after the Water of Life? "I am the water of life," He says. Are we stumbling in the darkness of sin and death? "I am the light of the world," He says. So also, "I am the door,—the way,—the truth,—the vine." Here, in an affirmation that embraces all these other claims, He says, "I am the resurrection and the life." Are we in distress of soul because our lives seem incomplete? Because we are missing the green pastures and still waters of the Psalm? Because sin and death are assailing us at every turn? Are we seriously concerned about the outcome of the mortal conflict between life and death in our members and in the world about us? Do we really want to live? "I am the resurrection and the life," says Jesus; "Here it is, take it!" He is both willing and able to work His miracle of resurrection in us here and now; we need not wait until the end of the age.

Certainly, all who know Him by more than hearsay will tell you that He is not merely concerned about the rehabilitation of the personality in the dim, distant future. He is also concerned about the redemption and reintegration of the personality here and now. It is sin that destroys life. It is sin that disintegrates personality. It is sin that brings death to the soul. By His death on the cross the Lord of Life has provided a solution of the problem of sin in our lives. By His death on the cross He has "abolished death and brought life and immortality to light." By His death on the cross He has opened to us the doors to eternal life, the life of God. We need but let Him take the place of self in us, and eternal life will be ours here and now; and it will be ours forever!

III

Our third thought is but a continuation of the second. The Christ whom we worship is also *our Life in the world to come.* Listen to His words: "He that believeth in me, though he were dead, yet shall he live, and whosoever liveth and believeth in me shall never die." The dust must return to the dust from which it came; but the life we share with Christ, our life in Him, lives on and on, every atom of it, in the bosom of the Father. In this world it is life in the midst of death, but it is nevertheless the gift of God, the work of God in us. Therefore it continues to be life after our mortality has returned to the dust. Freed at last from the limitations of the flesh, from all that separates us from God, it can now come to full flower and bloom.

"But how can these things be?" we ask. Well, for one thing, the life Christ offers us is the work of God, and because it is the work of God, it is eternal, as eternal as God. It is too precious to perish with the body. People sometimes ask, "Is the eternal life Jesus offers us present or is it future?" The answer is, "It is *neither* and it is *both.*" That which is eternal cannot be either present or future; it must be both. It transcends time. Therefore it also transcends the dissolution of matter, what we call the death of the body. Most of us have observed that nature guards all her creations with a jealous eye, using every atom of matter and every ounce of energy over and over again, so that nothing is ever lost. Is it reasonable to suppose that, of all the things God has made, the life of one of His children should alone be subject to extinction? Is it reasonable to suppose that a reasonable God would save wood and hay and stubble and then let life, individuality, and personality go by the board?

Then, too, our Lord has taught us that the name of God is Father, and if God is our Father, is it reasonable to suppose that He would allow death to come between Him and us? "Immense have been the preparations for me," writes Whitman. Is it reasonable to suppose that our Father God would put so much into His preparations for us and then cast us from Him as a child discards a plaything? Is it reasonable to suppose that He would tire so quickly of His children and surrender them so wantonly to the oblivion of the grave?

The truth is, it is not only reasonable to believe in the

resurrection of the dead: it is manifestly unreasonable not to believe in it. It is the only faith that makes life worth living and service worth while. But this reasonable faith is not based upon reason; it is based upon Jesus Christ and the gospel that has grown up around Him. This gospel is the only argument in which we Christians have confidence, and it is not an argument at all; it is a revelation. As we study this revelation, and let it fulfill its mission to our souls, we learn to say with Martha, "Thou art the Christ, the Son of God," and when we have said that, we have said everything.

Yes, He is the Christ, the Son of God. Eternal life, the life of God, is as near us as He is. That He is both willing and able to share it with us is written all over the gospel. He who called Lazarus forth from an earthly sepulchre can also lift us out of the spiritual sepulchre which "we by our sins have deserved." He who conquered death on Calvary can also conquer death in our lives. He who rose from the dead can also work His miracle of resurrection in us. The sole condition is that we must be one with Him by faith. What will your answer be, my brother? You can take your place with those who used the raising of Lazarus as a pretext for intensifying their hostility to the Lord of Life. You can live your life without relation to Him, without thought for Him. Like the beasts of the field, you can carry on from day to day, intent merely upon your share of fodder and your place at the stall. If that is your mood and purpose, you will find that the life you have chosen will eventually turn to dust and ashes in your hands. But if, like Mary and Martha, you put your trust in Him who is the Resurrection and the Life, if you let Him take the place of self in your life, if you view every choice and every decision in the light of your relation to Him, striving earnestly to let Him control your life, the outcome is likewise sure. You will enter upon the life of God in this world, and the life of God is a life that cannot end. Eternal life or eternal death! That is the forced option that confronts us in our daily choices and decisions. May God help us to make every choice and every decision in the light of this forced option. We cannot have eternal life in the other world unless, by the grace of God, we begin to live it here and now.

QUINQUAGESIMA

Sons of Zebedee

Harry F. Baughman

QUINQUAGESIMA

AND James and John, the sons of Zebedee, come unto him, saying, "Master, we would that thou shouldest do for us whatsoever we shall desire."

And he said unto them, "What would ye that I should do for you?"

They said unto him, "Grant us that we may sit, one on thy right hand, and the other on thy left hand, in thy glory."

But Jesus said unto them, "Ye know not what ye ask. Can ye drink of the cup that I drink of? And be baptized with the baptism that I am baptized with?

And they said unto him, "We can."

And Jesus said unto them, "Ye shall indeed drink of the cup that I drink of: and with the baptism that I am baptized withal, shall ye be baptized: but to sit on my right hand and on my left hand, is not mine to give; but it shall be given to them for whom it is prepared."

And when the ten heard it, they began to be much displeased with James and John. But Jesus called them to him, and saith unto them, "Ye know that they which are accounted to rule over the Gentiles exercise lordship over them; and their great ones exercise authority upon them. But so shall it not be among you: but whosoever will be great among you, shall be your minister: and whosoever of you will be the chiefest, shall be servant of all. For even the Son of man came not to be ministered unto, but to minister, and to give his life a ransom for many."

—*Mark* 10: 35-45

Sons of Zebedee

And there came near unto him, James and John, the sons of Zebedee, saying unto him, "Teacher, we would that thou shouldst do for us whatsoever we ask of thee." And they said unto him, "Grant that we may sit, one on thy right hand, and the other on thy left hand in thy glory."—Mark 10: 35-37

WE expect the children of our worldly kingdoms to seek patronage and preferment from the princes and leaders whose battle they have shared. "What do I get out of it?" is the instinctive question of men like ourselves as we face the issues, the decisions, the opportunities of life, and relate ourselves to the leaders and movements that claim our loyalty.

But when the children of the Heavenly Kingdom are found with the same unsanctified ambition in their hearts we are a bit shocked. It seems out of place for the Sons of Zebedee to appraise their relation to Christ in the characteristic human phrases, "Do for us;—Grant unto us."

To be sure, James and John may not be too harshly condemned by any modern disciples for making this request of Jesus. For they were thinking of the Kingdom of God exactly according to the pattern of their time. Experience and the illuminating power of the Holy Ghost had not yet taught them the real nature of their Master's Kingdom and their own place in it. When most of the people of their day thought or spoke of the Kingdom of God they had a very definite picture upon the screen of their minds. It was a picture of a conquering champion and deliverer throwing off the hated Roman yoke, restoring the throne of David, and ruling with power and glory from Jerusalem, with rich patronage and honor to bestow upon his courtiers.

"They all were looking for a king
To slay their foes and lift them high."[1]

Because these two disciples shared this expectation, and because they were men possessed of human desires and motives and ambitions they believed they had the right to seek the chief portfolios in the government they expected Jesus to set up at Jerusalem, especially since they had cast in their lot with Him from the beginning. Accordingly, dazzled by the prospect of place and preferment, and moved by the human love of rewards they made their plea, *"Do for us;—Grant unto us."*

Looking upon this scene, hearing the self-interested proposal of the disciples, and the heart-searching reply of Jesus, "Can you drink the cup I shall drink; are you able to be baptized with my baptism?" we are impressed by the contrast between two fundamental conceptions of the religious life.

I

On the one hand there was the religion of the Sons of Zebedee. These two disciples were destined one day to achieve

[1] "That Holy Thing"—George MacDonald, in "World's Great Religious Poetry." Page 327.

a more pure, spiritual motive and consecrated service. But at the moment of this request they were thinking of their relation to Jesus as a way of promoting their own interests. It may be that their thought of rewards had in it some measure of eternal, spiritual quality. It is more likely that what they coveted was place and distinction in a kingdom they expected here and now. But whatever the outlines of that kingdom were for them, they felt that their fellowship with Jesus must result in a tangible, satisfying reward.

This conception of religious value plagued the whole ministry of Jesus. He constantly encountered the "Sons of Zebedee." Religion is a bargain with Heaven. Men standing on the street corners to pray that they might be praised for their piety; men sounding a trumpet before them as they gave their alms, that they might receive the reward of a reputation for generosity; people being fed with the loaves and fishes one day, and on the next following Jesus, expecting a repetition of His miracle until He, recognizing their shallowness and self-interest, exclaimed sadly, "Ye seek me not for my sake but because ye did eat and were filled." These all were of one spirit with the Sons of Zebedee. They thought of their relation to Jesus primarily in terms of recompense. The fellowship He established was all but wrecked upon that desire for reward, as the disciples quarreled again and again over who should be first in the Kingdom, like men who must be guaranteed a gilt-edged investment, before they will take the risk.

Religion has always had its "Sons of Zebedee," those who think of it as a way of advancing their own interests, and gaining their own ends. One of the oldest pieces of drama in Scripture, the book of Job, contains this appraisal of religious motive —incidentally by Satan, but alas too often true—*"Doth Job serve God for nought?* Hath he not prospered on every side? But stretch forth thy hand and touch *that which he hath,* and he will curse thee to thy face." And one of the Psalms sings complacently, if not adventurously, "I will praise the Lord because He hath dealt bountifully with me."

Our own religion has not been entirely free from this sort of motive. The "Sons of Zebedee" are still to be found. "Do for us,—Grant unto us," we have continued to say. Henry Van Dyke, in his story, "The Mansion," makes Mr. Wightmen's son say, after his father has discouraged his altruistic desire to serve mankind in unnoticed ways, and urged upon him a greater prudence, "I can see it already, sir, and the way you describe it seems amazingly wise and prudent. In other words, we must cast our bread upon the waters in large loaves, carried in sound ships, marked with the owner's name so that the return freight will be sure to come back to us."[1] That speech summarizes many a man's attitude toward religion, and indeed the attitude at times of the Church itself. We have seen religion employed as the bulwark of privilege and the buttress of power to maintain conditions favorable to the strong and the fortunate until in sheer revulsion from its own selfishness men have written over a once stately Christian temple the inscription, "Religion is the opiate of the people." In one ancient country after another in recent years the Christian religion has been under fire, and when you search the history of the Church in those coun-

[1] Van Dyke, "The Mansion," Charles Scribner's Sons.

tries you discover that it has been saying by its conduct—"Do for us,—Grant unto us."

The religion of many of us as individuals has shared this attitude, and no doubt we have all had at times within our souls something of the spirit of the Sons of Zebedee. We think of religion in terms of contract rather than adventure. We approach it with the all too human question upon our lips—"What do I get out of it?" We do not always choose Christ for His own sake, but, like the multitude of old, follow Him for the loaves and the fishes, or their modern equivalent. Religion that is shrewd calculation, that has its eye chiefly upon the reward—"Grant unto us"—is something less than Christ's religion.

II

Contrasted with this religion of the Sons of Zebedee is that pure, spiritual, sacrificial dedication which speaks in Jesus' reply to the two self-interested disciples, "Can you drink my cup, are you able to be baptized with my baptism?" Any religion that is worthy the name must live in the spirit of that speech. One reason that religion has suffered so much in the eyes of the world is that it has too frequently had in it so much of self-interest. Too many men have thought of it and used it as a sort of insurance or investment. They have made it their "Safety First," and have known nothing of the Saviour's fiery test of true religion, the ability to drink bitter cups and to be baptized with hard baptisms.

The Sons of Zebedee were transformed by the grace of Christ and the power of His Spirit until they became in deepest and fullest reality sons of God—"Beloved now are we the sons of God, and it doth not yet appear what we shall be." And the first lesson they learned in this experience was that only by sharing the sacrificial life of Christ did they become members of His Kingdom. Their religion was no longer a self-interested seeking of the coveted seats, but a self-burying dedication to Christ and His cause. They no longer said, "Do for us whatsoever we ask of thee," but "Do with us whatsoever thou wilt for thee."

This is religion at its highest and only true expression. It is always dedication, and, at its best, means sharing Christ's cup and baptism. The most inspiring pages of Scriptures are those which record the lives and experiences of men whose religion was of this order. Thus a man like Job after many hard and bitter experiences answers the sneer of Satan with his speech of triumphant faith, "Though he slay me, yet will I bless him." A man like Habakkuk facing the bitterness of life with the agnostic's question on his lips comes finally to a victorious faith and sings in clearest strain, "Though the fig tree shall not blossom and there shall be no fruit in the vine; the labor of the olive shall fail and there shall be no meat in the field; the flock shall be cut off from the fold and there shall be no herd in the stall, yet will I rejoice in the Lord and joy in the God of my salvation; and I will walk with him in heavenly places." A man like St. Paul exclaims, "I count all things but dung for the excellency of the knowledge of God in Christ Jesus." Men like these have sought no measurable reward, but in their self-forgetting dedication have found life's true reward.

One of the stories related of St. Thomas Aquinas tells us that as he was in prayer and intense meditation upon the things of Christ a voice, which was that of his Master, spoke to him and said, "Thomas, for all thy labors and thy service unto me, what reward wilt thou have?" And Thomas renouncing all desire for any of the treasure the mind of man might covet, lifted his eyes toward heaven and exclaimed, *Nihil, nise te, O Domine*—"Nothing except thyself, O Lord." The soul that has found Him and is found in Him needs no other reward. The Sons of Zebedee possessing this treasure may say, "Now are we the sons of God." And dedicated souls will sing with St. Francis Xavier—

"My God, I love Thee—not because
I hope for heaven thereby—
Nor yet because, if I love not,
I must forever die.

"For me to lowest depths of woe
Thou didst Thyself abase;
For me didst bear the cross and shame,
And manifold disgrace.

"Then why, O blessed Saviour mine,
Should I not love Thee well?
Not for the sake of winning heaven,
Or of escaping hell:

"Not with the hope of gaining aught,
Not seeking a reward—
But freely, fully, as Thyself
Hast loved me, O Lord!

"E'en so I love Thee, and will love,
And in Thy praise will sing;
Solely because Thou art my God,
And my eternal King."

Francis Xavier, 1542
Tr. Edward Caswell, 1848

ASH WEDNESDAY

A Preview By Caiaphas

John L. Deaton

ASH WEDNESDAY

THEN gathered the chief priests and the Pharisees a council, and said, "What do we? For this man doeth many miracles. If we let him thus alone, all men will believe on him: and the Romans shall come and take away both our place and nation."

And one of them, named Caiaphas, being the high priest that same year, said unto them, "Ye know nothing at all, nor consider that it is expedient for us, that one man should die for the people, and that the whole nation perish not."

And this spake he not of himself: but being high priest that year, he prophesied that Jesus should die for that nation; and not for that nation only, but that also he should gather together in one the children of God that were scattered abroad.

Then from that day forth they took counsel together for to put him to death. Jesus therefore walked no more openly among the Jews: but went thence unto a country near to the wilderness, into a city called Ephraim, and there continued with his disciples.

And the Jews' passover was nigh at hand: and many went out of the country up to Jerusalem before the passover, to purify themselves. Then sought they for Jesus, and spake among themselves, as they stood in the temple, "What think ye, that he will not come to the feast?"

Now both the chief priests and the Pharisees had given a commandment, that, if any man knew where he were, he should shew it, that they might take him. *—John 11: 47-57*

A Preview By Caiaphas

Ye know nothing at all, nor consider that it is expedient for us, that one man should die for the people, and that the whole nation perish not.—John 11: 49, 50

AN Episcopal rector, with a keen sense of humor, was talking one day to a group of his own people. He was discussing Lent. Whimsically but poignantly he said: "Lent is the time when we Episcopalians hunt around among our sins for a few which we can conveniently give up for forty days."

I fear that is all Lent means to many of us. We trim an indulgence here, add a religious observance there. We increase our usual offerings by a few pennies a week. We may say a few more prayers. We, perhaps, read a little out of our unused Bible. And that is Lent.

Why not lift Lent out of the category of legalistic observance and make it what it ought to be above all other things—a time of increased fellowship with Christ? We are commemorating a period when our Lord was living more and more intimately with His Heavenly Father, so that His life could be a mounting crescendo of love and service, so that He would not be alone when forsaken by all others, so that at last He could be lifted up on Calvary as the Saviour of men. Only as we follow the pattern of His life will Lent be able to fulfill its highest purpose in our lives.

The Gospel selected for this day ushers us at once into the very heart of the Lenten message. It sets before us in faint outline the supreme experience in the passion of our Lord, and particularly suggests the purposes to be accomplished by it. It is most interesting to observe that this preview is given by one who was a bitter enemy of Jesus, whose avowed ambition was to frustrate His ministry and to effect His complete destruction.

Events were rapidly approaching a crisis. The healing and teaching ministry of Jesus had always been a matter of some concern to contemporary religious leaders, but so long as He confined His activities to regions somewhat remote from their headquarters they were not unduly disturbed. Now He had come to their very doors to work a miracle of sensational interest. In near-by Bethany He had restored Lazarus to life under circumstances that left no shadow of doubt about the genuineness of the miracle. The whole community was astir. The story was upon the lips of every person, and the conviction was growing in many hearts that there was sound basis for His claim to Messiahship.

Caiaphas and his associates were now truly aroused. Their hearts were filled with the hatred of the ecclesiastic whose soul is dead, who welcomes no new movement in religion which does not emanate from the official class. They were convinced that something had to be done immediately to check this wave of nascent enthusiasm. Further delay and toleration would endanger the security of their own positions. The time had come for final and decisive action. So a hasty meeting of their highest ecclesiastical council, the Sanhedrin, was called to deal with this emergency.

John gives us a glimpse of their growing apprehension, revealed by their deliberations. Their language suggests men who feel the ground giving way under their feet. "What are we doing, for this man doeth many miracles? If we let him thus alone, all men will believe on him: and the Romans shall come and take away both our place and nation."

What a contrast between Jesus and His enemies! He moves with the confidence, quietness and certainty of one who knows what He is doing and where He is going. His enemies are panic-stricken; they flounder around in the dark trying to find some charges to justify, in the eyes of the people, their diabolical desires. They must not reveal their true concern. Perhaps they can cover it with the cloak of patriotism which is so often the refuge of the scoundrel and unscrupulous man. "The Romans will come and take away both our place and nation."

In the midst of their discussion, the voice of their President rings out. He will hesitate and vacillate no longer. His mind is made up and he presents his solution with authoritative conviction. Thus Caiaphas achieves the terrible distinction of having first suggested publicly the death of Jesus. John speaks of him as prophesying. Is it possible that the spirit of this man, at a moment when he is plotting a heinous crime, could be under the directing influence of the Divine Spirit to such an extent that he expresses a blessed truth and foreshadows a great event of divine administration? We find it difficult to believe that Caiaphas, at this moment, could possess any divine illumination, not even like that which enabled Balaam to foresee the future prosperity of Israel. Rather does it seem to be a case of unconscious prediction, an instance in which God "makes the wrath of man to praise him." His words are comparable to the jest of the crowd around the Cross, "He saved others, himself he cannot save"; or the inscription which Pilate ordered placed over the Cross, "This is the King of the Jews." All are words of divine wisdom, but spoken without discernment. Yet, in spite of the character of the man, we must admit that the Divine Spirit used the savage utterance of this crafty schemer to set forth the nature and power of Christ's death, and thus give a preview of His passion.

As we reflect upon his words, we observe first his emphasis upon the necessity of the act. Ye know nothing at all, nor consider that it is expedient for us, that one man should die for the people." That little phrase, "for us," betrays the speaker and reveals his appreciation of the necessity. He was concerned about what Jesus and His ministry would do to him and his kind, and well he might be. Jesus made it unmistakably clear that He was deadly opposed to all religious bigotry and to all exploitation of the human race in the name of religion. His scorching words to the Pharisees and His attitude toward the money changers in the temple left no doubt on either score. This touched a tender spot in the life of Caiaphas. He was the personification of all that is base and despicable in a corrupt clergy. Under the guise of religion he carried on a racket that would compare favorably with the Roman heirarchy in the days of Luther and would make our modern radio "free lancers" look like novices. Jesus would lift religion to a much higher level. He would break the shackles of legalism and deliver men into the glorious liberty of the children of God. His message had struck a responsive chord in the hearts of a people weighed down with grievous burdens. Caiaphas knew what that meant. The handwriting on the wall left no room for doubt. Either he or Jesus would have to go. There could be no compromise. With eyes totally blind to the beauty of the character of Jesus, to the truth of His saving message, to the proof of His Messiahship, he could see nothing but the security of his priesthood and his own personal fortune. In the light of that vision, there could be only one verdict: Jesus must die and be put out of the way once and for all time. The real justification which he felt for this rash proposal was couched in these words, "It is expedient for us."

For an altogether different reason, Jesus recognized the necessity of the Cross. He saw it as a part of God's plan of redemption for man. From the very beginning of His ministry, He had been etching the Cross on the horizon so that His disciples might understand and be prepared for it. The somewhat veiled expressions first used soon gave way to clear and positive statements. "He began to shew unto his disciples that he must go unto Jerusalem . . . and be killed." The emphasis always seems to be on the "must." For Him Calvary would not be an accident nor a blunder on the part of foolish men. It was not to be forced upon Him by any human power. Not even all the Roman legions could take Him against His will. He would lay down His life in harmony with the divine plan. The necessity was from above and from within.

There will always be the element of deep mystery about the necessity of the Cross. We may spin our theories of the

Atonement and try to explain the "why and wherefore," but when all is said, we must finally fall back upon the word which declares that it "thus behooved Christ to suffer." It was the requirement of divine wisdom and love. Love and the Cross are inseparably linked together. That ought to satisfy us.

We turn to the words of Caiaphas again and we note his suggestion of the vicarious character of this sacrifice. "It is expedient for us that one man should die for the people, and that the whole nation perish not." Of course this was only subterfuge. The real interest of Caiaphas was not the people nor the nation, but himself. He was merely employing the favorite scheme of politicians, ecclesiastical and otherwise, to further his own ambitions. His proposal must take the form which will enable men to act upon it with the feeling that they are carrying out some great moral principle rather than indulging their own passions. The Fascists tried to enthuse their fellow men with the cry, "We will build a new empire." Likewise the Nazis shouted, "We are building a greater Germany." All they succeed in doing is losing their empire, restricting and impoverishing their Germany, and strewing the bodies of their enthusiastic followers like offal across the battlefields of the world. So Caiaphas would pose as the defender of the people and the saviour of the nation, but the ultimate result was the destruction of the Jewish nation, the degradation of his people, the defamation of his own name. By the time John wrote these words, the catastrophe which was to have been prevented was brought about by the very act which Caiaphas proposed, and the High Priest had become the patron saint of all those unprincipled rascals who like to use moral platitudes to promote their wicked plans. Nevertheless, he did state, unwittingly, a blessed and glorious fact about the death of Jesus. It was a vicarious act. He died for all people and the salvation of all nations.

There are many problems whose solution is difficult for man. Efforts to prevent war and promote lasting peace meet with one failure after another. Attempts to adjust the economic life of society so that the well-being of all shall be served are not conspicuously successful. These and similar problems we do not put in the class of the hopeless and impossible. We believe there is a way out if man will use his best ability under divine guidance. But there is one problem which man can never solve for himself. He can never remove his sin nor effect his own salvation. He must allow God to do that for him. The vicarious sacrifice of Christ alone makes it possible.

We do well to remember the word of Paul in 2 Cor. 5: 21: "He hath made him to be sin for us who knew no sin; that we might be made the righteousness of God in him." Our sins were placed upon the sinless One and in His death they were nailed to the Cross. He did what no one else can ever do: He destroyed sin. It was not His sin; it was ours. His death was vicarious.

We are passing through days which recall to us a story which came out of World War I. A group of English soldiers were exposed to a wave of poison gas as they crossed "No Man's Land." When the sergeant was overcome by the noxious fumes, the lieutenant ran to his aid. Just as help came, the young officer himself was overcome, fell backwards into a shell hole and broke his neck. When the sad news reached the parents in north of England, the mother said, "I feel that the only thing that would console me for my loss would be to know that the man for whom my boy died was a good man." A short while later this very sergeant, hopelessly intoxicated, came to the home of that mother. It was soon evident that it was not a case of sudden temptation but rather a habitual way of life. After his departure, the mother spoke again, "It almost breaks my heart to know my boy gave his precious life for a worthless life like that." But what of the young officer himself? He knew this man; he was a member of his platoon. Yet knowing him, he gave his life in the attempt to save him.

One cannot hear this story without recalling Paul's words: "For scarcely for a righteous man will one die; yet peradventure for a good man some would even dare to die. But God commendeth his love toward us, in that, while we were yet sinners, Christ died for us." His death was unique and incomparable. It was completely vicarious. None of it was for Himself; all was for others.

We turn to the words of Caiaphas again and we find a third aspect of the passion of Jesus brought to our attention. "He prophesied that Jesus should die for that nation; and not for that nation only, but also that he should gather together in one the children of God scattered abroad." He proclaimed the unifying and rallying power of the death of Christ. Contrary to every desire of his heart, he set forth Jesus as the true paschal Lamb, whose blood would atone for the sins of the world, and whose death, by abolishing sin, would re-establish the unity of the human race.

Jesus Himself declared, "And I, if I be lifted up from the

earth, will draw all men unto me." Nothing could be more typical of the history of Christianity. Whenever and wherever the Cross has been exalted before men, He has drawn them unto Himself. Thinking men, who honestly face the problems of life, are attracted by Him. They find in Him the answer to the deepest questions of life which relate to human conduct and destiny. Likewise suffering humanity is drawn to Him as to no one else. He alone gives refuge and strength, rest and peace in sufficient measure. Above all, those who sin find in Him forgiveness. He lifts the burden of guilt and breaks that bondage which binds us to present and future sins.

And by the very act of drawing us to Him, He draws us to each other. "The children of God that were scattered abroad" were all to be united around that Cross. To bring mankind together in some semblance of brotherhood has long been one of the major problems confronting the world. Modern inventions and modes of travel have almost annihilated space and time and made the world one neighborhood, but this has not resulted in greater peace and harmony among men. Our very proximity has become the occasion of increased rivalry and friction.

Men may well ask the question whether there is an effective unifying power to be found on earth. There are still those who believe that humanity can be held together only by the power of the mailed fist. Make the nation or combination of nations so powerful that all opposition can be immediately crushed by those who hold the reins of authority. One glance at the world, one brief survey of history, tell the story of horror and failure which this philosophy has wrought. Others look to racial ties, national bonds, continent or hemisphere welfare, economic interests, etc., to achieve this objective, but it is a vain look and a forlorn hope. Permanent and satisfying unity simply does not come through such forces alone.

Over against these is the method suggested in our Gospel. Caiaphas was thinking of a narrow, racial unity and he was most insincere about the method, but notwithstanding his blind hatred and sinister purposes, God used him to proclaim a principle which has universal application. It is the unifying power of the Cross. Here we find a dynamic, which once released, will transcend and overcome all the divisive forces which rage in the world. When men are really at one with God through the atoning sacrifice of Christ, they must be at one with each other. God willing, we shall soon be attempting to heal the ghastly wounds of war and trying again to build a peaceful world. Many plans are already being evolved to show how we can build "One World." We believe that the Cross of Christ with its unifying power has the greatest contribution to make to this most difficult problem.

As we begin another season of Lent, we do well to reflect upon the profound words which came from the lips of one who spoke more wisely than he understood. We do even better to accept the challenge to quicken and intensify our fellowship with Christ that we may understand more fully the meaning of the Cross—its necessity, its vicarious character, its rallying and unifying power. Let us put the Cross where God wants it to be. Make it the center of our deepest desires, our most fervent hopes, our highest ambitions. We shall find our own lives enriched, and we shall help transform the life of the world.

INVOCAVIT

The Uncompromising Christ

George J. Gongaware

INVOCAVIT

FROM that time forth began Jesus to shew unto his disciples, how that he must go unto Jerusalem, and suffer many things of the elders and chief priests and scribes, and be killed, and be raised again the third day.

Then Peter took him, and began to rebuke him, saying, "Be it far from thee, Lord: this shall not be unto thee."

But he turned and said unto Peter, "Get thee behind me, Satan: thou art an offence unto me: for thou savourest not the things that be of God, but those that be of men."

Then said Jesus unto his disciples, "If any man will come after me, let him deny himself, and take up his cross, and follow me. For whosoever will save his life shall lose it: and whosoever will lose his life for my sake shall find it. For what is a man profited, if he shall gain the whole world, and lose his own soul? Or what shall a man give in exchange for his soul?"

—*Matthew 16: 21-26*

The Uncompromising Christ

For whosoever will save his life shall lose it; and whosoever will lose his life for my sake shall find it.
—Matthew 16: 25 (16: 21-26)

CHRIST demands a full surrender. The text admits of no doubt on this point. A half-hearted devotion to Him is worthless. He refuses it, because it is treason! The present-day regimentation of men for military service, each man pledging loyalty to his leaders, and his life, if need be, to the cause of the freedom involved, is an impressive illustration of the necessity for an "All-out" for our Country's flag.

The "Four Freedoms," today so warmly approved, are not a new gospel. They are intimately related to the Gospel of Christ. Each one of them is instinct with the meaning of Christ's own Word. They are worthy of notice; each one of them is here emphasized by an apt passage of Scripture. You, dear reader, will want to cite other passages. Here they are—

Freedom of Religion

God is a spirit, and they that worship him must worship him in spirit and in truth.—John 4: 24

Freedom of Speech

Ye shall receive power after that the Holy Ghost is come upon you; and ye shall be witnesses unto me both in Jeru-

salem and in all Judea and unto the uttermost part of the earth.—Acts 1: 8.

Freedom from Want

I was an hungered and ye gave me meat.

—Matthew 25: 35 *et seq.*

Inasmuch as ye have done it unto one of the least of these my brethren, ye have done it unto me.—Matthew 25: 40.

Freedom from Fear

Be of good cheer, I have overcome the world.

—John 16: 33

Lo, I am with you alway, even unto the end of the world.

—Matthew 28: 20

If God be for us, who can be against us?—Romans 8: 31

The Gospel for this Sunday is a further proof of the basic authority for these freedoms which are much more than a political creed. They declare a spiritual crusade and are a call to arms. They define the social gospel of the whole New Testament and point the great goal which God has set for man and toward which the human spirit has struggled through the ages.

Here is a challenge to an "All-out" for Christ, and to a new faith in God's message for the final and full realization by all men of His good will and purpose for mankind.

Jesus was ever alert with His challenging, all-in-all message. Out and onward He now goes in the face of bitter foes; into the jaws of death He goes conquering and to conquer by that spiritual power which always proves invincible.

This Gospel is preceded by a dramatic dialogue; it is introduced by a prophetic prologue. Jesus said to His disciple, "Behold I go up to Jerusalem and all things that are written concerning the Son of man shall be accomplished." This prologue is followed by another dramatic dialogue between Jesus and His disciples—

Jesus speaking—"At Jerusalem I shall suffer and die and the third day rise again."

Peter speaking—"This shall not be unto thee."

Jesus speaking—"Get thee behind me Satan; thou mindest not the things that are of God, but those that be of man." Hear it again: "For whosoever will save his life shall lose it; and whosoever will lose his life for my sake shall find it; for what is a man profited if he shall gain the whole world and lose his own soul, or what shall a man give in exchange for his soul?"

Man is free and safe only when he is bound to God and by God, and for God and man. The Uncompromising Christ is our title, and this much can be said here for that full surrender which Jesus taught to Peter and to the other disciples, and which His Gospel is teaching to us again today, namely, that no man is a true Christian who is not bearing His Cross; that man must know Him and must follow Him, or life is a bitter disappointment, and "the game is not worth the candle"; and that this is true of men and of nations as well.

The text is both generic and specific. The inescapable question, pointed and personal, is, "Shall we be safe and successful and happy in His service, or Shall we be daring and defiant and defeated and dead in opposing it, yea, even in neglecting it? There is no other alternative.

It all breaks down to this,—we can follow Christ only by faith and with a cross. Rather it adds up to this—no man can serve two masters; and Christ demands and deserves our best—our all! The only way to save one's life is to lose it in Christ, and there is no worldly profit sufficient to compensate for the loss of one's heavenly heritage.

Men think of God, recognize God; men seek and follow Christ from one of three motives:

CUSTOM—CONVICTION—CONSECRATION

From Custom:—Have you ever thought of churchgoing, for example, as a habit? It is that. A fixed habit in individuals often establishes a community custom, and for a man to recognize God, and the opportunities for service of God and man, from the force of general custom alone is better than nothing. A good religious habit is better than no habit of worship at all. It is infinitely better than a bad habit. He is wise who is willing to learn from the example of others; and many a faithful Christian has been credited with preaching sermons as long as from his own front porch to the church door simply because people have observed his ways. But mere custom may prevail dominantly with an individual and in a community, and yet many a soul be utterly unfed, utterly asleep, utterly forgotten, and utterly lost!

From Conviction:—When a man can say with St. Paul, "I know whom I have believed," he has reached a fine intellectual basis, but when he can add with St. Paul—"and am persuaded," he has reached one of the finalities of faith! Let every man be fully persuaded in his own mind (Romans 14: 5). That is infinitely better than simply to follow the crowd. When a man knows definitely and surely the principles of salvation through Christ and His Gospel, and when he faithfully observes them he is on a much stronger basis than is the man who has only made a guess or is simply influenced by the direction in which the crowd is moving. Custom is as sand. Conviction is as bed-rock. Man must find a sure foundation. Only then does he reach that high plane that leads him to a still higher and deeper and safer relationship to God and man.

It comes by Bible study, meditation, and prayer; by public and private worship, and by the right use of the Means of Grace, the Word and the Sacraments; and how sure that makes the mind, and how trustful the heart becomes, and how sweet and meaningful is that intimate relationship between the individual and his God!

From Consecration:—Neither custom nor conviction is sufficient of itself. Even though they be united they are still inadequate. Jesus is here trying to have Peter and the other disciples, and you and me, also, come to a full surrender of body, mind, and spirit to His Gospel in its full meaning and import. To a respect for custom? Yes! To an appreciation of the importance of conviction? Yes! But to something that is deeper and stronger and more permanent; to something that is unshakable; to something that even the gates of hell cannot destroy. To something that is immortal and eternal and invisible because there is in it the purpose of God's mind for the world, and Christ's eternal sacrifice for the sin of mankind; to something that calls for the administration to the believer's inmost soul, by Word and Sacrament, of the Grace of God; to something that produces a spiritual growth that is so increased as that eventually all the resources of omnipotence are available to him, for his life is saved by its being lost in Christ.

Custom alone makes a slave. Conviction alone makes a fanatic; but Consecration—the yielding of every faculty and every power that man possesses to the will of God, to the Grace of Christ, to the mercy of our Heavenly Father—that's Consecration, and with that God is well pleased and mankind is served and the individual is eternally blessed!

To respectfully observe custom; to renew penitently and daily one's convictions, and constantly seek to deepen the measure of our consecration until we come to the fullness of faith and to the knowledge of the Son of God and the full stature of life in Christ Jesus,—these are the steps in the way that leads to eternal life!

That's the lesson of Today's Gospel. That's the message of this text and that's the call and the technique that emphasize the importance of the Lenten Season, wherein this blessed end must again be diligently sought daily.

The best elements of custom and conviction and the entirety of consecration constitute the Christian's hopeful endeavor and cheerful response to the challenge herein contained. It is repeated to us with new significance today by the Uncompromising Christ! It is this that results in the constant growth of that inward and inmost thing that we call

Faith, and faith is more than the solution of an intellectual problem. It is this that makes possible a total surrender. It is this that helps the believer to possess the things that abide. Herein are found the enduring treasures, and here alone the soul comes into possession of the eternal values, namely, the presence and the grace and the power and the peace of God which passeth all understanding. Now, as ever, Christ is the Way, the Truth, and the Life! Amen.

REMINISCERE

Names Written in Heaven

Paul Wagner Roth

REMINISCERE

AND the seventy returned again with joy, saying, "Lord, even the devils are subject unto us through thy name."

And he said unto them, "I beheld Satan as lightning fall from heaven. Behold, I give unto you power to tread on serpents and scorpions, and over all the power of the enemy: and nothing shall by any means hurt you. Notwithstanding, in this rejoice not, that the spirits are subject unto you; but rather, rejoice because your names are written in heaven."

—*Luke* 10: 17-20

Names Written in Heaven

OUR Lord appointed seventy disciples to engage in a great missionary enterprise. Having instructed and empowered them, He sent them "two and two before his face, into every city and place, whither he himself would come." Presently they return, wildly excited by their successes and rejoicing that "even the devils are subject unto us through thy name."

Their glorying is not good. The Lord reminds them that success is a dangerous thing, especially when it rests upon the wrong foundation. Unless corrected, they may soon begin to "sacrifice unto their own net, and burn incense unto their own drag." They think too much of themselves and their own personal powers, too little of what is infinitely more important. They lay more emphasis upon "subject unto us" than upon "through thy name." Discerning their danger through temptation to spiritual pride and self-righteousness our Lord says to them, "Notwithstanding in this rejoice not that the spirits are subject unto you; but rather rejoice, that your names are written in heaven."

Even disciples may fall under the dominion of the devil through their very joy that he is subject unto them. They may come to despise those who have been less successful, or denounce them as deficient in zeal and good works,—as did certain Pietists in our own Lutheran Church two centuries ago. They may mistake personal power for spiritual status and forget that even graceless men may be employed, for the time being, in promoting works of divine grace in the hearts of others.

To desire a good name is most natural. We all want to do something that will cause us to be remembered. So deep-rooted is this desire for an imperishable name that history records the lives and deeds of many who did evil, deliberately, in order that their names might be remembered. One burned down the temple of Diana at Ephesus. Another changed the course of the river of an ancient city and slaughtered twenty-two thousand of its inhabitants. Another caused thousands of slaves to dig a canal with their bare hands and boasted how many he had destroyed by this brutality. Again and again, a "world-shaker" strides across the scene of human history, reckless and ruthless in his ungodly ambition to make a great name for himself. The builders of Babel (ancient and modern), always say, "Go to,—let us make us a name."

A modern writer observes that "one strange result of scientific progress has been the reversion of monotheism to local idolatries"; which prompts another to say that "when those" local idolatries "are not state and race and class—which are the self writ large—then they are just personal self." No wonder our Lord is concerned to deliver His disciples from pride and self-worship. Pride is the great sin. In other vices the devil works through our animal nature. Pride, however, does not come through our animal nature at all. It comes direct from hell. "In this rejoice not that the spirits are subject unto you, but rather rejoice, that your names are written in heaven."

"Names written in heaven"—what does it mean? We know, of course, that this is a poetical expression common in Scripture; but what does it mean in plain prose? How is it brought about? Who does the writing, and when, and where, and how? Of what value is it to have one's name written in heaven, and is there anything we can do about it?

It is a great thing to have one's name written in the New Testament. Of this we are sure when we read the genealogies in the Gospels, the rollcall of the Christian brethren in the last chapter of Paul's Letter to the Romans, the hero-chapter in the Letter to the Hebrews. It is a great thing to have one's name written in the Family Bible or, now that the old Family Bible has become a museum piece, on the tablets of the hearts of godly parents. It is a great thing to have one's name inscribed in the Parish Register and on the Roll of Communicant Members. And now that we are deep in the war the Honor Rolls are being posted everywhere—names written in appreciation of our boys who are doing and dying in defense of all that we hold dear and of our girls who are in active services. But to have one's name written in the Lamb's Book of Life is greater than all these. Indeed, this is the greatest thing that can happen to any human being. Ages ago the wise man wrote, "A good name is rather to be chosen than great riches, and loving favor rather than silver and gold." If it is a great and good thing to enjoy the loving favor of one's fellow men what must it be to enjoy the lovingkindness of Almighty God! "Then they that feared the Lord spake often one to another:

and the Lord hearkened, and heard it, and a Book of Remembrance was written before him and them that feared the Lord, and that thought upon his name"—(Malachi 3: 16).

Of what value is a good name if it is not somewhere indelibly inscribed? Archaeologists spend their lives digging up and deciphering ancient records, some chiseled in stone, some cast in bronze, some written on papyri and parchments. Libraries are filled with records, state and city archives are bursting with them:—and all the while "the gnawing tooth of time" is obliterating them so that whole peoples, their civilizations, their learning, their great names and golden deeds are lost to us forever. Horace once boasted, "I have erected a monument more lasting than brass, loftier than the pyramids." He thought his poetry was immortal. But who reads Horace today? When war and its aftermath have done to death our Liberal Arts schools, our young bachelors of science and technology will scoff, "Who is Horace?—and so what!" Because she once ruled the waves Britain boasted that she had a "name written in water." Now, however, the task is to write the nation's name in the air—the least stable of all things on which to write one's record. Not so with God. His records are imperishably preserved, not in time but in eternity. Endless and infinitely better are His ways of writing. Men have guessed that "the tendency of character is toward permanency," and the prophet of God reminds us that what we do is recorded in the sum total of what we are. It already begins to be legible in our faces,—"The show of their countenance doth witness against them." But St. John tells us of certain saints whose greatness was stamped upon them by other hands than their own:—"And I looked, and lo, a Lamb stood on the mount Sion, and with him an hundred and forty and four thousand, having his Father's Name written in their foreheads." Isaiah knows of another place where God keeps His records:—"Fear not, for I have redeemed thee, I have called thee by thy name: thou art mine. . . . Behold I have graven thee upon the palms of my hands."

What a place for your name to be written! In the pierced hands of Jesus! In the Lamb's Book of Life! Have you listened to the little Salvation lassie singing on the street corner? "At the Cross," and "When the Roll Is Called Up Yonder"? She sings and rejoices because her name is written in heaven. Have you thrilled at the singing of the great congregation on Whitsunday when the Confirmation Class enters the church? Their hearts are in the singing because their names are written in heaven. When First Church observes its Golden Jubilee the founding fathers and mothers and all the charter members are celebrated because their names are written in heaven. When mourners carry the ashes of their dead to the cemetery their grief is assuaged because, through their tears, they have a vision of One who said, "I am the resurrection and the life: whosoever liveth and believeth in me shall never die."

And when times are evil, as they are today, the saints still rejoice. They remember that He must reign, till He hath put all enemies under His feet. The enemies of God may march roughshod over all that is holy, but God is never finally defeated. They rejoice and sing because the victory is already won in Christ Jesus and, although for a time they are called on to be partakers of Christ's sufferings, they know that when

His glory shall be revealed they shall be glad also with exceeding joy. The noisy laughter of the fool, the frothy mirth of the worldling soon turn to weeping and wailing; but the child of God, though his eyes be filled with tears, may nevertheless have a heart throbbing with joy. St. Peter tells us that the Apostles and primitive Christians were filled with "joy unspeakable and full of glory,"—and that was in a time of persecution! Think of Paul and Silas singing for joy down there in that dismal prison! The inward blessedness of the friends of Christ breaks forth in paeans throughout the New Testament and continues to this day in an endless Alleluia because they "know whom they have believed and are persuaded that he is able to keep that which they have entrusted unto him against that day."

The child of God has endless reasons for rejoicing, but how does the name of an earth-born man ever come to be written in heaven? There is an immense, dark and perplexing region surrounding Regeneration through which we can make our way only after the new birth has taken place. "I cannot by my own reason or strength believe . . ." The denial of the necessity for being born from above is the very essence of God's controversy with the natural man. Why a man should not be able to grow better and better until at last in his own right and by his own hand he inscribes his name in the Book of Life and inherits the Kingdom is beyond the man in the street and the philosopher in the school. But to the children of God this is really as absurd as to ask why a stone should not grow more and more living until at last it becomes a man. "Except a man be born again he cannot see the Kingdom of God." If he cannot see it how can he desire it, and how can he enter that which he does not desire and cannot even see? From the side of the natural man there is no way by which he can cross the great gulf between that which is born in sin and that which is born of God. The difference between these two is a difference not of growth but of birth. To become sons of God we must be born of God, have something of our Heavenly Father within us, stand in a new relationship to Him, receive a new essence and a new nature. John must have been profoundly interested and influenced by what he learned of the conversation between Jesus and Nicodemus on the subject of Regeneration, for, years later, he writes, "Beloved, now are we the sons of God, and it doth not yet appear what we shall be: but we know that, when he shall appear, we shall be like him." The mystery is too great for us, but we know a man cannot "born" himself. The first movement comes from God and we love Him because He first loved us. It is He who writes our names in heaven.

Such high spiritual birth and status carries with it great privileges and responsibilities. We are under strongest obligation to live up to our new station in life. The man in Christ must manifest Christ. "Holiness unto the Lord" must be upon the bells of the horses, and upon the pots in the Lord's House, and upon the frontlet of the servant of God. There is no reason why the Christian should not have his horses, his automobiles, his many gadgets, but "Holiness unto the Lord" should be engraved upon them! What about amusements? Enjoy them if you can, but write upon them "Holiness unto the Lord." If they stand up under that all is well. Otherwise they bear the mark of the beast.—Well, all this may seem to throw us back upon our own efforts if we hope to have our names written up there. But that is not so:—it is just another wording of the paradox which St. Paul encountered in his own Christian experience:—"Work out your own salvation in fear and trembling, for it is God which worketh in you both to will and to do of his good pleasure."

Paul gained his great name—a name written in heaven if ever there was one—by being crucified with Christ and rising in newness of life. No longer is the old, proud, self-righteous Saul in control of his life and work. It is a new man who says, "I am crucified with Christ: nevertheless I live, yet not I, but Christ liveth in me: and the life that I now live in the flesh I live by the faith of the Son of God, who loved me and gave himself for me." Thus, as the result of his new birth and his boundless faith in Christ, it came about that Paul's name is second only to the Name that is above every name in heaven and on earth. There is no self-salvation or perfectionism in all this—nothing but the free grace of God. To keep us humble our daily life reminds us too frequently that we have this heavenly treasure in an earthen vessel!

Individual and social salvation belong together, but for too long a time now emphasis has been placed upon the social aspects of Christianity. Individual salvation has come to be regarded by too many as a higher form of selfishness, and religion today is preoccupied with civic righteousness, the elevation of the masses, the impending social crisis, and all manner of such relative things. Without disparaging this interest in human welfare may we still be permitted to observe, that now is the time to bring home, in direct and personal manner, the burden of our text:—Is YOUR name written in heaven?

Jesus' method was to press through temporal to eternal values, to break through the individual's guard until He reached his conscience. His message was never left up in the air, it always struck home. His disciples were trained in the same method. Andrew finds his own brother, and brings him to Christ. Peter goes right after Cornelius. Philip leaves the crowded city for a lonely road and gets into the chariot with the Ethiopian eunuch. Paul talks to saving purpose with his jailor. Apollos has a great Bible class in Aquila and Priscilla. And so we find abundant warrant in Scripture for our emphasis upon personal salvation. We press the question, Is your name written in the Book of Life? The disciples would have asked you that! Can you answer it?

We may know, yet we dare not presume. If you believe and are baptized according to Christ's command; if you love the Lord, and His Word is your delight; if you love the Lord's people and the worship of the Lord's House, and hunger and thirst after righteousness; if you love your neighbor as yourself and strive daily to live in peace and helpfulness in all your human relationships,—then you may be sure that something is at work within you which is not of the flesh but of the Spirit. "You may not be able to name the day of your birth," said Moody, "but you can know for sure that you are born." God's Spirit bears witness with our spirit on this question, and brings us joy and peace in believing what His Word and promises declare. Bengel, in his commentary, has this for us, "How can one know whether his name is written in the Book of Life? . . .

Only look to it that thou ever hold faithful to the name of the Lord Jesus Christ; for the rest let Him take care."

Can I do anything to help write others' names in heaven? Read the Book of Acts and learn, in the very first chapter, that we are to receive power from on high to become witnesses for Christ even unto the uttermost part of the earth. And in the next chapter the power is given, Peter preaches, and three thousand souls are added to the Church! The book is full of the wonderful things that Jesus began both to do and to teach, and He still does wonders through those who abandon themselves to Him and His will. The blood of the martyrs helped write names in heaven. The prayers of the saints, the work of the missionaries, deacons, deaconesses, preachers, teachers, parents—who shall tell the story of their helpfulness in bringing sinners to God? Even the little children may serve in His plan for the ingathering of souls. Yes, we can help write names in heaven. "Go ye into all the world and preach the Gospel to every creature."

"Saviour, if of Zion's city
I, through grace a member am,
Let the world deride or pity,
I will glory in Thy Name.
Fading is the worldling's pleasure
All his boasted pomp and show:
Solid joys and lasting treasure
None but Zion's children know."

The Steadfast Face

William C. Schaeffer, Jr.

OCULI

AND it came to pass, when the time was come that he should be received up, he steadfastly set his face to go to Jerusalem, and sent messengers before his face: and they went, and entered into a village of the Samaritans, to make ready for him. And they did not receive him, because his face was as though he would go to Jerusalem.

And when his disciples, James and John, saw this, they said, "Lord, wilt thou that we command fire to come down from heaven, and consume them, even as Elias did?"

But he turned, and rebuked them, and said, "Ye know not what manner of spirit ye are of. For the Son of man is not come to destroy men's lives, but to save them."

And they went to another village.

And it came to pass that, as they went in the way, a certain man said unto him, "Lord, I will follow thee whithersoever thou goest."

And Jesus said unto him, "Foxes have holes, and birds of the air have nests: but the Son of Man hath not where to lay his head."

And he said unto another, "Follow me."

But he said, "Lord, suffer me first to go and bury my father."

Jesus said unto him, "Let the dead bury their dead: but go thou and preach the kingdom of God."

And another also said, "Lord, I will follow thee; but let me first go bid them farewell which are at home at my house."

And Jesus said unto him, "No man, having put his hand to the plough, and looking back, is fit for the kingdom of God."

—Luke 9: 51-62

The Steadfast Face

And it came to pass, when the time was come when he should be received up, he stedfastly set his face to go to Jerusalem.

WHEN the winter was passed, and the rain was over and gone, and the flowers appeared in Joseph's lovely garden, Christ died on the cross. But the stream that thus flowed to the flood had its rise in a distant day. Luke links these words of Christ's unswerving purpose with the transfiguration of many months before, and they only reiterate the will of a lifetime.

Christ had but one purpose. This brought Him into the world. "I came down from heaven, not to do mine own will, but the will of him that sent me." This was His daily bread. "My meat is to do the will of him that sent me." The secret of the cross hid in His heart swept Him unerringly to His end and goal and attainment.

Jesus knew what awaited Him. He knew that He would meet the cruelty and injustice that have always robbed men of their peace and security. He knew that He would overcome evil and hate only by becoming the victim of it and emerging through it. Through the centuries all who have suffered from ignorance and malice have looked at the steadfast face of Jesus and been strengthened and sustained. Now we know that the victories gained through force and violence are short-lived; that patience and forgiveness are more effective weapons than enmity and revenge. Jesus' fearless facing of the cross and its consequences is the unfailing source of courage and fidelity to all who suffer shamefully and wrongfully.

In our Gospel the disciples had scarcely started in the direction of Jesus' face, when they met with a rebuff. The Samaritans were in no mood to offer shelter to Christ and His company, and Jesus' followers wanted to call down fire from heaven to consume them. This is our way of treating intolerance and racial bigotry. Were Jesus' answer heeded now, our world would not every few years be kindled into conflagration. "The Son of Man is not come to destroy men's lives, but to save them." Our world's hope is, that Jesus, with set face, will keep marching to the music of His redemptive mission. As Stalker says reassuringly, "The life of Christ in history cannot cease. The dead nations are waiting till it reaches them, and it is the hope of the earnest spirits who are bringing in the new earth. Every development of juster ideas, of higher powers, of more exquisite feelings in mankind, are only new helps to interpret Him; and the lifting up of life to the level of His ideas and character is the program of the human race."

In the light of Jesus' set face then we learn that the Christian life is *purposeful.* It is meant to be thoughtful, but it is not meant to be weighed down with all sorts of scruples and hesitations which choke action. Jesus' invitation to men to share His mission called forth a courageous response which took all the daring men had. Jesus' presence and spirit seemed to sweep men to a decision. Those who were sunk in dreary self-absorption felt a new impulse and acted on it. The blind man cast away his garment with a new inrush of hope. The woman who had long been pushed aside now pushed right into the crowd to touch the hem of His garment. The woman at the well, languid enough, felt a new impulse to go to people and tell them about Christ. Matthew rose up from the receipt of custom and followed Him. Many of us need to recapture the sense of glowing life which Christ's influence awakens.

Too many people go through life seeking only inferior things. They live to get money, or to seek pleasure, or to win fame. Like the tortured Sisyphus of the Greek fable, they are forever pushing the round stone to the top of the hill, only for it to roll down again.

Thousands who seek the best never find it. They look only for the beautiful and precious things of this world. They get honor and learning and human love and human happiness and earthly success. But they do not seek God and they make no place in their life-plan for the Kingdom of Heaven. There is but one supreme good. We may have all else, but if we have not Christ, we are poor. We may have almost no other earthly good, yet if we have Christ, we are rich.

The easy way is not to trouble ourselves about the best things—spiritual attainment, unselfish service, winning others to faith. In the scheme of things, little premium seems to be placed on exhausting toil and costly self-sacrifice. But the love of Christ impels us to our holiest, our bravest, our best. The Master's face, set toward the cross, looks into ours and we know that we shall lose nothing by giving up for Him ease or pleasure or profit or life itself.

"O Master, point Thou out the way,
Nor suffer Thou our steps to stray;
Then in the path that leads to day
We follow Thee."

Christ's unhasting, unresting journey to Jerusalem opens for the Christian the road to peace and power.

Again, Christ's steadfastness teaches that *character* comes through the costliness of decision and effort. Even the Captain of our salvation was made perfect through suffering. For the joy that was set before Him He endured the cross. It was painful to Jesus to turn His back on the quiet scenes and tender associations of Galilee and turn His face toward Calvary. But this was the essence of His greatness, and in that choice He became the Saviour of the world.

No good work is easy work. Luther translated his Bible into the German language, and that translation is one of the great books of the world. But Luther said: "I sweat blood and water in my effort to render the prophets into the vulgar tongue. How difficult it is to make these Jew writers speak German." Sometimes he spent weeks in hunting out and meditating on the meaning of a single word. This wrestling with the ancient roots not only built a language of a new and richer flavor, but built a stauncher, robuster Luther to meet the crises of a day of destiny. Patience, constancy, courage, endurance and faith are qualities that are not conceivable except in connection with the difficult things in life.

Often we rebel against hard circumstances, saying that we

cannot accomplish anything because of them. But the fact is that in an easier lot we never could show what is in us because there would be nothing to put us on our mettle. Of some lives it is true that they never had a chance because they never had a hard job with all its rough edges which hook into a man's very being and catch hold of him like so many burrs until he is all one with it. The power of our obstacles may seem hostile and malign, but it is a power which goes over into us when we contend with them. Whenever we see another life which is marked by serenity, mastery, and grace, and begin to wish that our life had been better circumstanced so that it might have resulted like that, it would be better to wonder what particular and prolonged disadvantages that man had to conquer to acquire the grace he has.

As our first discovery of our own reality is made by the resistance of the things around us, which we touch and meet with infant hands until we come to a conception of the world outside of us and our place in it, so too it is hardship and difficulty and resistance that give us the growing sense of our own reality. We complain that we are not getting hold of things because of the hindrances we meet, when the fact is that by these things we get our hold. We are all for power, forgetting that we need friction quite as much as we do power. "A train of cars sustained in mid-air could not be budged an inch by the power of ten thousand engines. It needs the rails against which the wheels seem to groan and complain but which really give the wheels the only liberty they have to get anywhere." There is inspiration in difficulty that leads to spiritual power.

Again, Christ's steadfastness teaches us that life's purpose is *redemptive.* His set face looks beyond the cross to the new earth. He seeks to share all the fruits of His triumph and victory. Relief from all that we fear and attainment of all that we seek are His to give. The tragedy is that we look away from Him.

There are defections and disloyalties of faith. We are not capable of our full strength in Christ's cause because we are lacking in commitment and self-devotion to Him. By our love of Him we need to refute today's claim that religion needs to be released from dependence on any personality, however majestic. Our day's blasphemy is that our religion's progress is hampered and restrained by Christ's dominance of it. We answer, "No." All other persons may become tyrannies to us. Christ cannot. His service is perfect freedom. The more we know of Him, the more we become one with Him, the freer, richer, fuller our lives become. This great permanent Person is the key to our personality. He unlocks our best selves. Instead of suppressing individuality, He leads it forth. Wherever He goes the dull monotony into which the world cramps itself is broken into glad variety. With every new apprehension of Him the soul finds something new and joyous. Jesus is our religion.

This is our answer to the assumption that modern usage requires our Christianity to be "overhauled under the direction of scientific ideas of nature, human nature and history." What have naturalism, liberalism, humanism, to offer us beyond the heathen religions? Shall we continue weakly apologetic, while the basic foundation and the structural ideas of faith are undermined—God, Christ, the Bible, the Church, Revelation, Sin,

Salvation? Christ's steadfast face rebukes the spiritual invertebrates of our day.

The time is here for Christ's followers to demonstrate the power of the Gospel. Our world has just about been wrecked by man-made theories and speculations. As Dr. Speer has said, "Learned men write on the problem of life, striving to throw light upon it and to find its clue, and their books scarcely recognize the fact that Jesus ever existed. As for the idea that He has the words of eternal life, many modern philosophers scout the suggestion, and others who cherish it in their hearts do their work utterly apart from any contribution of Jesus to the solution of the problem of life." Because not everything that is true in faith and life can be explained to everybody's satisfaction, is no reason why what is true cannot be proved in its effectual working. Men and women everywhere who find in Jesus the way, the truth and the life, are given guidance and strength, under Jesus' empowering, to love God with all their mind and heart and their neighbor as themselves.

The world scene need not overwhelm us then while Jesus still sets His face and while we can look to Him. When Gen. Booth was asked the secret of his success he declared promptly, "God has had all there is of me. There are men with brighter minds, men with greater opportunities; but from the day I got the poor of London on my heart and a vision of what Jesus Christ could do with the poor of London I made up my mind that God would have all of William Booth there is. Whatever of power is in this movement is because God has all the adoration of my heart, all the purpose of my will, and all the influence of my life." That is it—looking to Jesus and in the direction

He looks, to the cross and beyond the cross to the redemption of the world.

In this sense, preaching is but witness to the Gospel. Looking into the upturned faces of people seeking the guidance and light of God's Word, what does one see? Strain and tension, doubt and unbelief, failure and defeat, hope and expectancy, all fan out in front of one who stands in the pulpit. George Wharton Pepper is right: "A glance at some of those eyes should be enough to stir your manhood to the core. 'O God,' you should inwardly ejaculate, 'give me at least a little that I may pass it on to them.' "

Little children, growing up in irreligion and amid surroundings hostile to growth and character, furnish the world's most fertile field for a mighty sowing of the Gospel. The chief treasure in any community is its children. At any cost their interests must be conserved and their future assured. For a generation the animal psychologists have been telling us that ideas do not influence behavior. The truth is that ideas and ideals mold character, and it is our first business to condition our children. Society does not seem to have any answer for the rising tide of crime except more money for jails, penitentiaries, and asylums. This is not the answer. There are homes and churches and schools enough in our land to save the children to a worthy mission and a proper destiny. Right motives, right training, right direction given to unfolding young lives carry the promise of a new order and a new day that can come no other way.

And when youth rises to opportunity, with due effort and responsibility, many ancient evils will be abolished. The very foundation of a richer and better life for all is that all shall be capable of wanting to share it. Increased leisure ought to be on the basis both of increased production and wise use of time, culturally and spiritually. For too long we have been too satisfied to live on the low level of physical comfort and cheap amusement. To fulfill the ideal of Jesus, wealth and power must cease being the badges of success; and at the opposite end we have to rise above the poverty, ignorance, lack of ambition, shiftlessness of character, and contentment with mean things that reduce so many to penury and want.

Indeed, were we really to set our faces, like Jesus' set face, toward the cross and the redeemed life beyond, we could rid our world of war and the ills and evils in its train. The way of peace for the nations is the way of forgiveness and amendment. The high ideals of a warless world, of international accord, of the autonomy of small nations, of the rights of minorities, of the guaranty of religous freedom are the ideals of Christ's religion, and they never will be brought about except through men and women who share His spirit and who are willing to venture and hazard all for His sake.

If men are allowed to despair of Christianity, the hope of a better world will perish. Freedom and democracy are but empty words without expanding opportunity and improved conditions which only character can bring about. Great anti-Christian nations of whole peoples have risen in our time, and there will be more of them *unless the Church again lives heroically, sacrificially.* Christ's divine unfailing perfection poured out from the cross alone can enable men to live together in love, to walk together in peace.

LAETARE

Bread of Heaven

Jeremiah J. Schindel

LAETARE

"VERILY, verily, I say unto you, he that believeth on me hath everlasting life."

"I am the bread of life. Your fathers did eat manna in the wilderness, and are dead. This is the bread which cometh down from heaven, that a man may eat thereof, and not die. I am the living bread which came down from heaven: if any man eat of this bread, he shall live for ever: and the bread that I will give is my flesh, which I will give for the life of the world."

The Jews therefore strove among themselves saying, "How can this man give us his flesh to eat?"

Then Jesus said unto them, "Verily, verily, I say unto you, Except ye eat the flesh of the Son of Man, and drink his blood, ye have no life in you. Whoso eateth my flesh, and drinketh my blood, hath eternal life; and I will raise him up at the last day. For my flesh is meat indeed, and my blood is drink indeed.

"He that eateth my flesh, and drinketh my blood, dwelleth in me, and I in him. As the living Father hath sent me, and I live by the Father: so he that eateth me, even he shall live by me."

—*John 6: 47-57*

Bread of Heaven

IT was a day in early spring when the Passover crowds on their way to Jerusalem followed Jesus to the other side of the lake, intent upon hearing His words and having a part in His ministry of healing. The day was far spent and Jesus was thinking of their bodily needs. "Whence shall we buy bread that these may eat?" He asks. Philip might have said, "Lord, Thou knowest"—but Philip was a realist; it would require fifty dollars' worth of bread for every one to have but a little, and they were sure of only five barley loaves and two small fishes. That was enough, just as the few bushels of seed grain sown are enough with God's blessing to produce the bounteous harvest. They did eat and were filled, but when Jesus perceived that they would come and take Him by force to make Him a king, He departed again into a mountain Himself alone. He was a different kind of King whose throne was to be the Cross.

The bread which Jesus came to give men was a different kind of bread, the Bread of Heaven. When the people discovered that Jesus had crossed the lake, they followed Him to Capernaum. Here He tells them that the bread He had given them the day before was not enough, that they must have the

Bread of Heaven. They reminded Him that Moses had given the people of his day such bread when God through him gave them manna from heaven. Would He be a prophet like Moses? The answer is, "I am that Bread of Life."

Henry Drummond wrote a book entitled, "Natural Law in the Spiritual World." He found plenty of material for it in the New Testament, especially in the teachings of our Lord Jesus Christ. The seed and the soil furnish such an analogy and the leaven and the meal. Our Lord finds the law of the spiritual life in the experience of the grain of wheat, which unless it falls into the ground and dies abideth alone. That was true of every grain of wheat which entered the flour to make the bread which we eat. We live from life and from life which was given for us. That is the law of the Cross, and the life which our Lord Jesus gave He gave for the life of the world.

God provides for everything that He has made the food that it needs. That provision is in accord with the kingdom to which the creature belongs. The plant lives from the mineral kingdom, the animal lives from the vegetable kingdom and from the animal kingdom. A monarch once visited a group of children in a school and pointing to his ring asked to what kingdom it belonged. The answer of course was, the mineral kingdom. He then pointed to the flower he was wearing and asked to what kingdom it belonged. The answer was, the vegetable kingdom. When he pointed to himself and asked, "To what kingdom do I belong?" he expected to be answered, The animal kingdom. A little girl in the group however answered, "The Kingdom of God." Man belongs to two kingdoms. On his animal side he lives from the vegetable and animal kingdoms, but on his spiritual side he lives from God. St. Augustine said, "Thou hast made us for Thyself, and our heart is restless, until it find rest in Thee."

Bread may be defined as the means of life. As such it mediates life. As far as the earth is concerned, its life-giving qualities must be mediated. We cannot live from the earth directly, but we can live from the plant which lives from the earth. That is our earthly bread,—but like the earth it is perishable. It is different with the Bread of Heaven,—if any man eat of this bread, he shall live forever. The Bread of Heaven is the means of eternal life because it mediates the life of God. They called the bread in the wilderness "manna," meaning "What is it?" It was mysterious. There is a resinous product of the tamarisk tree still called "manna," which may account for it. There is an edible lichen blown about by the wind which others think may be the manna referred to. That, however, does not account for how and when and where it came. The only thing that explains that is God. It is quite the same with our Lord Jesus Christ. He said, "I am come down from heaven," and the Jews said, "Is not this Jesus, the son of Joseph, whose father and mother we know? how doth he say, I am come down out of heaven?" In other words, there is a naturalistic explanation for the existence of Jesus Christ, but it does not explain all of the facts. The only explanation of the origin of Jesus Christ which is adequate is, that He is of God in a sense in which nobody else is, that He is the Son of God, the Living Bread which came down out of heaven, "True God, begotten of the Father from eternity and also true man, born of the Virgin Mary."

This Bread of Heaven must be eaten. That was true of the manna,—it is true of any kind of bread. Eating is as essential as bread itself; one might starve in the midst of plenty if he refused to eat or if for some reason or other he could not eat. There is something very personal and individualistic also involved in the act of eating. It is the individualization suggested in the Sacrament, "Given for thee"; "Shed for thy sins." If Jesus is the Bread of Heaven then it is true as He said, "Except ye eat the flesh of the Son of Man and drink his blood, ye have no life in you." This is done however by faith in Him, "for the words: 'For you,' require truly believing hearts." St. Augustine says, "Believe, and thou hast eaten."

Eating also means assimilating. God has not only provided bread for every creature but also the power to assimilate the life of that bread. In the physical world we speak of this as "metabolism," a very important bodily function. It is just as important a function in the spiritual world and just as essential to our wellbeing. To the plant God has given roots which reach down into the lifegiving soil and leaves through which it can take in the lifegiving elements of the air. He has not forgotten to do the same for our souls. God has not only given us the Bread of Life but also the power to assimilate Him, and that power is faith. But faith is something more than knowledge and assent, it is confidence. St. James says, "The devils also believe and tremble." They have knowledge but they do not have confidence. Faith without trust was not the faith of Abraham, it was not the faith of St. Paul. They knew the truth of God and they confessed it, but they also gave their hearts to God in confidence and obedience.

The earthly bread that we eat becomes part of our lives when we assimilate it; it gives us the physical strength to think and to speak and to act, it becomes one with us and we with it. When we assimilate the life of Jesus Christ, we abide in Him and He in us, we become one with Him, dead indeed unto sin but alive unto God through Jesus Christ our Lord. St. Paul was by faith so identified with Christ that he could say, "I am crucified with Christ: nevertheless I live; yet not I, but Christ liveth in me: and the life which I now live in the flesh I live by the faith of the Son of God, who loved me, and gave himself for me." That is eating the flesh of the Son of Man and drinking His blood. That is eating and assimilating the Bread of Heaven.

We must have physical bread in order to live physically. It is true of every earthly creature that in the midst of life it is in death. The destructive forces are continually at work and, if we do not build up our bodies as rapidly as the destructive forces tear them down, our health is impaired and death ensues. It is just as true that we must eat the Heavenly Bread that our souls may live. In the invisible world the destructive forces too are continually at work and if we do not build up what they tear down we can have no spiritual health. But Christ builds up what sin tears down. Sin destroys confidence in God, but Christ restores it. Sin destroys love to God and love toward man, but Christ restores both. Sin destroys conscience, but Christ restores it. Sin destroys communion with God, but Christ restores it. Sin destroys holiness, but Christ restores it. Sin, in a word, destroys life, but Christ restores it. He not only restores it, He sustains and nourishes it. He is not only the Medicine of the soul, He is the Bread of Life.

The fact of the life of the soul is quite as evident as that of the body. There are a number of simple tests by which the life of the body may be determined—respiration, pulse, and nerve reflexes. There is a similar way of telling whether one is spiritually alive—a sensitive conscience, a spirit of prayer, and a spirit of love. St. John speaks of this latter test when he says, "We know that we have passed from death unto life, because we love the brethren." There were three things that characterized the life of the Lord Jesus Christ: He was pained by the presence of sin and death, He was always conscious of the presence of God, and His heart ever went out in love toward others. It was a Frenchman who said, "Tell me what you eat and I will tell you what you are." It was said of the disciples that men took knowledge of them that they had been with Jesus. They were like Him because they had made His life their life.

"Bread of heaven, on Thee we feed,
For Thy Flesh is meat indeed:
Ever may our souls be fed
With this true and living Bread;
Day by day with strength supplied
Through the life of Him who died."

JUDICA

The Son of Man Glorified

Conrad Wilker

JUDICA

THEREFORE when he was gone out, Jesus said, "Now is the Son of Man glorified, and God is glorified in him. If God be glorified in him, God shall also glorify him in himself, and shall straightway glorify him.

"Little children, yet a little while I am with you. Ye shall seek me: and as I said unto the Jews, 'Whither I go, ye cannot come:' so now I say to you.

"A new commandment I give unto you, that ye love one another: as I have loved you, that ye also love one another. By this shall all men know that ye are my disciples, if ye have love one to another." —*John 13: 31-35*

The Son of Man Glorified

LIGHTED on our way by the Gospel for this day we enter into the Holy of Holies of the Passion History and behold

THE SON OF MAN GLORIFIED

What a sacred and blessed privilege it is to behold His Glory, the Glory as of the Only-Begotten of the Father, full of grace and truth, and to stand within the radiance of its light.

Judas may not enter here, nor any who love darkness rather than the light. He had deserted the family circle of the disciples and sold his birthright in the Kingdom of Christ, for a mess of pottage.

His departure was the signal for the powers of darkness to set in motion their nefarious plans, but for Jesus it was the chosen hour to pour out His great heart to His faithful friends while He revealed to them His secret joy and laid upon their believing hearts His new and great commandment. Heavenly Wisdom dictated the choice of this hour, in which the hearts of the eleven were depressed by sorrow and foreboding, to strengthen and fortify their faith and to bind them more closely together in the bonds of mutual love. And so, while the powers of darkness gleefully anticipate their brief hour of power, Jesus

Himself, in that little circle of friends, but in the full view of the Father, reveals

The Secret of His Ultimate Triumph

The note of triumph and joy in the voice of their beloved Master is not lost upon the disciples even though at the time they did not comprehend its meaning. John, the beloved disciple, remembered it well. And all they who behold in the Son of Man only the Man of Sorrows acquainted with grief, need, by this scene in the hallowed Upper Room, to be instructed that He is above all else the triumphant Saviour who never lost sight of His ultimate victory. His is ever that victorious Kingdom against which the gates of hell can never prevail. Seeing this, even now, we may take heart again.

In this hour of grim darkness without, all is light within the Son of Man—for, said He, "Now is the Son of Man glorified, and God is glorified in him."

Strange words, these? No, it is but natural that in the hours immediately preceding his death, any son of man should search his soul and his life and through sincere repentance find forgiveness and thus be prepared to meet his God. But the Son of Man, who once had challenged His bitterest foes to convict Him of sin, now found in Himself nothing meet for repentance —only the sublime consciousness that God was glorified in Him.

Would we see God's brightest glory; we must look in Jesus' face. In thought, in word, and in deed, He was ever intent upon the Father's will. To His enemies He said—"Verily, verily, I say unto you, The Son can do nothing of himself but what he sees the Father do; for what things soever he doeth, these also doeth the Son likewise" (John 5: 19). To the Jews who marveled at His knowledge and wisdom, He said—"My doctrine is not mine, but his that sent me" (John 7: 16). But you, and I, who remember so well the very keynote of the gospel, voiced in the familiar lines—"God so loved the world, that he gave his only-begotten Son, that whosoever believeth in him, should not perish but have everlasting life" eagerly take to our hearts the precious signs of His love even as His beloved disciple has recorded them, as he beheld in them the glory as of the Only-Begotten of the Father. As we look through the eyes of John we behold the Father's love glorified in the Son of Man who entered into the joy of the home in the marriage at Cana and who, in the same little town assuaged the grief of the nobleman and the family circle, by restoring a beloved son. Compassion upon man, like that of the Father, ever companied with Him and manifested its power to break the bonds of sin, to feed the famishing multitudes, to calm the tempest tossed and fear-filled souls of His disciples, to give sight to the blind, to shed its tears at Bethany and to restore the dead to life. As in His deed so in His words we see the Father's love revealed. Who can fail to hear the Father's voice in the precious truths He has committed to our faith: "I am the bread of life," "I am the light of the world," "I am the door," "I am the good shepherd," "I am the resurrection and the life," "I am the way, the truth, and the life," "I am the vine, ye are the branches."

Truly, in Him was no sin at all—only grace and truth. He came not to destroy men's lives but to seek and to save the lost —to glorify God. And now the hour was fast approaching in which He would glorify God to the uttermost in that sweet sacrifice which is supremely Divine and so utterly unselfish and filled with love, that He could say of it: "And I, if I be lifted up, will draw all men unto me." Oh, it was not of compulsion by the powers of darkness, but for the joy that was set before Him, that He endured the Cross, despising the shame. Even before it came to pass it was a fact accomplished because He had determined to glorify the will of God.

Soon He would enter upon that joy—for "straightway God would glorify Him" with the glory which He had with the Father, before the world was. Soon, very soon, the portals of Heaven would swing wide, and He, the King of Glory, would enter in—to sit at the right hand of the Father. All power would be given to Him, in heaven and on earth, and He would say to His disciples even these few—"Go ye into all the world and disciple all nations." All of this and more—much more than we can possibly comprehend—entered into the secret joy of His heart in that hour of revelation and glory—the joy that sustained the Son of Man in the awful anguish of His Passion and Death—even in the dread hour when He cried—"My God, my God, why hast thou forsaken me?"

But what of these sorrowing and bewildered disciples, who hung upon His every word, though they understood Him not? One thought was in their hearts, one question was trembling upon their lips. He had read it and knew that presently Peter would ask it: "Lord, whither goest thou?"

Faithfully He had answered that question when He revealed to them the secret of His joy—but the immediacy of their sorrow at His departure (when or how they did not know), had numbed their understanding. Even so the urgency of our grief sometimes despoils us of the comfort of all divine promises. The where and the why of the Saviour's leading often become the mystery of sorrow.

But His love is ever patient and kind. Tenderly He devotes Himself to their perplexity. "Little children, yet a little while I am with you." Let us make the most of that little time. What a wealth of love is revealed in that term of endearment, which, according to the gospel records, was used but once by Him, but which became a favorite term of love in the letters of John. His heart went out to them in deep compassion. He knew the intensity of their love and how great would be their sorrow even though in the matter of a few days—it would be turned into joy. But such is the love of Jesus for His own, that even their temporary griefs command His compassion. But love is faithful as well as kind. Compassion must company with truth, though it cause pain. "Whither goest Thou?" you ask in your hearts. I tell you, that where I am going, you cannot come. And we know what He meant. He must tread the winepress alone. There is a sacrifice of love which only the Son of Man could make. Though they be willing to die for Him—yet that cannot be. He must die for them, or else they would ever seek Him in vain. He must go before them to prepare a place for them in order that after a little while He might receive them unto Himself. Yes, they would after a season, be glorified in Him also; but in the meantime they must glorify Him by their mutual love.

So while He does not remove the cause of their sorrow, the certainty of separation remains; yet in their mutual sorrow they would find consolation and comfort in mutual love. So a common sorrow draws hearts closer together and makes it easier to bear.

Yet they would continue to seek Him and He did not say that they could not find Him. Indeed they would find Him nearer to them than ever before; as they yielded their hearts in cheerful obedience to

His New Commandment

Was it a new commandment? O yes, quite new. It gave new meaning to the great commandment they knew so well since they had known Him and understood His interpretation of it. "Thou shalt love the Lord, thy God, with all thy heart" —how new it became to them when they knew for a certainty that Jesus was glorified in Him. How new it would be for Thomas after he had learned to say from the heart—"My Lord, and my God." Is it new to us because Jesus is in God—Jesus whom we know? If the commandment is still quite impersonal then we do not yet know Him, whom to know is everlasting life.

And the second part of the great commandment, like unto the first, would be glorified by the new commandment which embodied within it the truly new and divinely vital element—"As I have loved you, that ye also love one another." How great and wonderful was the love of Jesus for His own—truly, "greater love hath no man than this, that a man lay down his life for his friends."

How then does this read: "Thou shalt love thy neighbour as thyself"? Would they henceforth be satisfied with that standard of self-love, "as thyself"? Would Peter ever dare to ask again "How often shall my brother trespass against me, and I forgive him: is it enough seven times?"

Was this "as thyself" the measure and standard of the Saviour's love to them and indeed to all men? Was He not compassionate, forbearing, patient, forgiving? Did He not lay down His life for the brethren? So must their love be henceforth—and ours. And yet there is a hidden and precious meaning to the new commandment. It is this—"that ye love one another." That meaning is not general but specific. Like the Saviour Himself, they and we must continue to love our neighbour even with a surpassing and unselfish love. We must also love our enemies as Jesus did, but in a very special sense and way, must we love the brethren.

Sometimes it would seem as if this special significance of the new commandment had escaped us. So little is said of the reality of the Family of Christ, of the special relationship that exists between the members of the Family, the Church, of which Christ is the Head.

There was a special urgency inherent in the new commandment. It was so needful in the early days of the Christian Communion, when all the world was against the followers of Jesus. Necessity was upon them to hold fast to each other in the bonds of love and hospitality. And it is worthy of special note, that in those days the Church prospered. Was it because they truly loved one another, even sight unseen?

Has that urgency passed away in our day when the world is no longer persecuting the Church and martyring Christians?

Perchance the world has gotten into the Church and corrupted it with its own spirit to the extent that many Christians have become philanthropists rather than Christian brethren. It is so much easier to make a confession of love than to practice it, particularly in our relations to the unlovely brethren. It is so much easier to make an occasional condescending contribution to a worthy cause, than to be faithful in Christian fellowship and brotherly love. Yet it is only by true faith, and Christian fellowship and love, that the Christian Church can hope to prosper and to win the world for Christ. Christian love reaches out to the unknown, the brethren of the other fold, and loves them sight unseen in the Spirit of Christ.

This is true Christian evangelism. Only they can love as Jesus loved who are His in very truth. Such love alone can impress and persuade men. That is why Jesus added the inviting assurance and promise—which also embodies the second direction in which we can glorify Him—

"By this shall all men know that ye are my disciples, if ye have love, one to another."

How Men Recognize the Presence of Jesus

Not for a moment would I minimize, even to the faintest degree, the necessity of fidelity to the truth as it is in Christ Jesus, or loyalty to the Christian creed, or devotion to confession of that faith in worship and service and conduct of life; but all of this will fail of its effect if there be no heart of Christian love.

"We know that we have passed from death unto life because we love the brethren," said John (1 John 3: 14); and by the same token, "He that loveth not his brother abideth in death."

In the light of this commandment dare we apply this test to our own souls? And how shall Christians know one another and commune one with the other in Christ? There is a common language spoken by all true believers, regardless of race or clime—the language of brotherly love. By it we speak in many tongues the wonderful works of God. By it we carry the gospel to the uttermost parts of the world, and by it the world is redeemed.

Even the world outside the Christian community did recognize Christ in His disciples. "How these Christians love one another"; said they, or this—"Their Master makes them believe that they are brothers." Yes, to know the fountain we must look at the stream. "By their fruits ye shall know them."

Are we known of all men today as Christians because we love the brethren? Are men attracted to the Church most of all because they see how its members love one another? So it ought to be, we all admit.

Truly, the love of Christ constraineth us to love one another as He loved us, in the same spirit, the same principle, and with the holy motive, that by so doing we may glorify Him, and that He at last may glorify us in Him.

Truly, the Spirit, who beareth witness with our spirit that we are the children of God, ever waits to bestow upon desiring hearts this firstfruit of love.

Let us therefore earnestly desire and cultivate this grace of love, that Christ may be glorified in us, and that we may "show forth His death until He come."

"Jesus, truest Friend, unite
  All Thy consecrated band,
That their hearts be set aright
  To fulfill Thy last command." Amen.

PALMARUM

The Recklessness of Christian Discipleship

Paul Hartzell Krauss

PALMARUM

THEN Jesus, six days before the passover, came to Bethany, where Lazarus was which had been dead, whom he raised from the dead. There they made him a supper, and Martha served: but Lazarus was one of them that sat at the table with him.

Then took Mary a pound of ointment of spikenard, very costly, and anointed the feet of Jesus, and wiped his feet with her hair: and the house was filled with the odour of the ointment.

Then saith one of his disciples, Judas Iscariot, Simon's son, which should betray him, "Why was not this ointment sold for three hundred pence, and given to the poor?" This he said, not that he cared for the poor; but because he was a thief, and had the bag, and bare what was put therein.

Then said Jesus, "Let her alone: against the day of my burying hath she kept this. For the poor always ye have with you; but me ye have not always."

—John 12: 1-8. (*See also Matthew 26: 6-13; Mark 14: 3-9*)

The Recklessness of Christian Discipleship

RECKLESSNESS! The very word alarms the prudent, offends the calculating, and disturbs the devoted. Yet from the world's standpoint, it accurately describes Christian discipleship. When the Christian offers his life to Christ he does it with a complete devotion, without reckoning the material values which make up life's meaning for the worldly mind.

Let us see this authentic characteristic of Christian discipleship, sadly missing in the Church today, illustrated by a new Palm Sunday Gospel. We are all familiar with the old one, with its rejoicing multitudes, its chanted Hosannas, and its waving palm branches. That is a picture of popular honor to Christ the King,—but it is touched with sadness. How short-lived is the glory of the world's acclaim; how sudden the change to the tragedy of Calvary! Let us, this Palm Sunday, refresh our minds and hearts with another picture. It, too, stands at the beginning of our Lord's last week. It, too, is bright,—but with an unfading glory. It is the story of a perfect, a "reckless" devotion. It is touched with beauty and fragrance, and warms our hearts and makes us glad for it, as we think of the pathos, the pain, the mockery, and the injustice which followed.

You know the story. On the evening of the Passover,—the last earthly Passover in the life of our Lord (for by the next Passover His body will be resting in its borrowed tomb), His friends of Bethany make Him a supper in the house of Simon the leper. Simon was there, Martha,—mistress of the serving, doubtless,—Mary, and Lazarus, quiet and wide-eyed with the wonder of his walk through the valley of the shadow of death. Judas, too, was there, and the disciples, a friendly company of some fifteen or twenty of the friends and followers of Jesus, just at the beginning of the great week of suffering. Just to remember that fellowship is pleasant. Our faith is no ascetic thing of hermit isolation. The love of Jesus enriches, multiplies, and makes beautiful everything that is good in life, both material and spiritual, both temporal and eternal. But that which crowns the occasion with a glory never to be forgotten, was Mary's deed of reckless devotion. Sensing the approaching climax, with a woman's intuition apprehending the suffering and the death that were to come, quickly she brings her most prized possession, an alabaster box of ointment and, after the custom of the Orient, breaks it in anointing tribute on the head and feet of the Saviour. It was the outpouring, the spontaneous, uncalculating expression of the spirit of love, and to express that devotion, nothing less than the best would do.

It was a costly gift. It represented a year's wages for the average workman, so immediately there was criticism. The wise, the prudent, the careful, were disturbed, Judas, particularly. "Why," he asks, "was not this sold and given to the poor?" There is heard the voice of the natural man, the protest of the fearful and the earth-bound. "Such a fund," they say, "could have been invested, and a committee established, and a New Economic Plan adopted, to solve the problems of poverty in Bethany and thereabouts!" From a practical, business, material standpoint it was a reckless waste. Yet Jesus praised it as a deed of supreme value, as worthy of eternal remembrance. If we Christians can only see the reason why, and catch the spirit which animated Mary, we will find new joy and power in our discipleship, the world will behold a new radiance in the Christian religion, and will feel the power which can again "turn the world upside down."

I

Mary's deed is a beautiful memory, which redeems the Holy Week story with a ray of light, because her devotion was uncalculating. She was "all out" for Christ and His cause. She wanted to honor her Saviour and she brought the best she had. That is the only kind of devotion which counts. A devotion which bargains on a temporal basis is not Christian. Our discipleship fails and the Church fails, and the coming of the Kingdom lags, when we are only half committed. We propose a limited service. It is the *Judas spirit* creeping into our discipleship.

Note how swiftly the world's criticism came, prompt to the deed: "Why was not this ointment sold for 300 pence and given to the poor?" He felt this way because he was materially-minded, selfish,—and dishonest. The world sympathizes with the question because it is enslaved to material things. Judas and his sympathizers think the world is to be saved by clever management of material, economic values. In that respect he belongs to the school which today believes that by the manipulation of material values the Golden Age can be guaranteed for all mankind. They think that by a socialistic or communistic or other political scheme, by proper laws and the organization of economic machinery, human beings can work out a good society. When will such "humanitarians" and "utilitarians" realize that always at the heart of every human scheme the naturally selfish soul of man must be reckoned with? It is the heart and soul that need some regenerative miracle, which will make it love to serve God and to sacrifice for the sake of brother-man. Only a miracle of Grace can do that. Such a miracle can be performed by the Spirit of Christ alone. Without that changed heart and soul, there is little hope of anything but perpetual strife in human affairs. But with that miracle of Grace in our hearts, we shall love our fellow men truly, with divine "recklessness" and faith. Let us plan, with every skill and wisdom we possess, to set up the machinery of human brotherhood. But as we do it, let us remember that only men possessed by the Spirit of Christ can make it work.

Mary's pure devotion, which is a reflection of the devotion of the Cross of Calvary, must come in and purify the poisoned atmosphere of its hate and envy. The world's greatest problems are not problems of material supply but of motive. They are not problems of economic poverty but of greed and envy and hate. They are the problems that Judas represents. The solutions rest with Mary, and her Master, Christ.

The Christian is not deaf to the prayers of the poor. On

the contrary, in the long run, Mary will do better by them than Judas ever did. Judas was not only materialistic, he was selfish and dishonest, and his question was a piece of hypocrisy. As we are told, he held the bag and was a thief. His complaint was an excuse, concealing a half-committed heart. The half-committed heart too easily finds an excuse for selfishness. Too often the innate selfishness of the soul finds expression under the smoke-screen of what we call practical prudence and sane business caution. "O, I never give to Foreign Missions. It seems so foolish when there is so much to be done here at home." Have you ever heard a statement like that? But how often that is voiced by those who give neither to Foreign Missions nor very much at home! It is the spirit which looks upon a lovely altar or a painted window in the House of God and protests complainingly, "What a waste of money!" Or, when out of devotion to serve the Kingdom a congregation proposes to raise a House of God, in which the utmost shall be done for the Highest, objection is made to such "waste," under the plea that such offerings should be given to the "poor."

The very charity for which Judas pleads itself can become a Christ-less thing if it have not the Christian motivation of love. Modern charity, with all its elaborate machinery, with the opportunities it provides for writing checks and making contributions, but with hearts unwarmed by contact with human suffering, is in danger of such soullessness. It is in danger of what John Boyle O'Reilly had described, too severely, perhaps, but with some justice, as

> "Organized charity, scrimped and iced,
> In the name of a cold, statistical Christ."

Mary of Bethany spoke the language of an unselfish love, and the fragrance of her devotion filled not only the room with its beauty, but has blessed the world ever since. She "anointed his body for the burying." Her heart sensed the opportunity for a grace-filled service. *Hers was a timely service,* when it counted most. Out of prudence, how often we delay, or out of mistaken reserve, to express our love and affection to those about us. Christian discipleship will not postpone its sacrifice until some other time. Christian discipleship will do all it can, *now.* Mary paid her tribute and warmed the heart of the Master with her affection before it was too late. Nicodemus and Joseph of Arimathea honored Jesus, after He was gone. Honorable and gracious as that was, they might have helped more had their help been earlier. Nixon Waterman has put this lesson into a lovely verse:

"A rose to the living is more
Than sumptuous wreaths to the dead,
In filling love's infinite store,
A rose to the living is more,—
If graciously given before
The hungering spirit is fled,—
A rose to the living is more,
Than sumptuous wreaths to the dead."

When Jesus praises the deed of Mary He corrects the world's selfish judgments. He stresses again the one value that counts, life dedicated in loving service. Self cannot come to greatness until it forgets self. That is the divine "recklessness" of the Christian, and, strange eternal paradox, as self is forgotten in devotion to the Highest, the soul "comes alive" and at last lives. "He that loveth his life shall lose it, and he that loseth his life for my sake shall keep it to life eternal."

II

Mary's offering was not only an offering of pure unselfishness, but it was perfect. It was perfect because she did her best. "She did what she could." Christ asks for all of us, and for all that we are, at our best. Here was this treasured gift of costly ointment. Without hesitation it was offered as a gift to the Lord. It was a personal gift because it represented life itself, the highest she had,—"what she could." In this gospel there is no light disrespect of material values. They have their place in our human economy. They represent blood and sweat and tears. They are the coinage of life. The alabaster box of spikenard was valuable as a visible symbol of life, life's effort, life's work itself. Mary wanted to symbolize the outpouring of herself. So she brought the grandest thing she had. It is an entrancing picture of pure devotion, as charming as a little girl shyly bringing her dearest doll to give to a friend in an impulsive act of love.

Christ asks you, who may be confessing Him for the first time on this Palm Sunday, to give yourself, all of you, all through life. If Christians generally were animated by this spirit the whole work of the Kingdom would immediately be transformed. No longer would Christians ask, "How much must I give?" but always "How much can I give?" No longer would they say, "How much do you think I should do?" but

"How can I make all of my life a larger service for the cause of Christ?"

Mary, without hesitation or calculation, seeing her opportunity and inspired by love, "did what she could." There are so many Christians who belong to the ancient and not-too-honorable order of the "O-if-ers." They say, "O, if I only had a million dollars I would give it to the cause of Christian Education"; "O, if I only could I would support a missionary in Africa"; "O, if I only had the gift of speech I would be glad to lead that class of young people." There *is something* everyone can do, for every life possesses talents. You have something for which God is waiting, which will exalt Christ. Give it. Pour it out. No one lives but has blessings which God who gave them is waiting to have used for Him. "The poor," Jesus said, "always ye have with you." Humanity has been created with varying degrees of skill and differing talents, but all are equal before God in the possibility of loving service, and the test which really counts is, Are you doing what you can?

As Christians, we ought to ask ourselves, Are we truly giving our lives to Him, or, Are we bargaining with Him and holding back reserve areas of self-indulgence? Are we ready to do what He wants us to do, and to go where He wants us to go, and to be what He wants us to be? That is characteristic of the great servants of the Church throughout the ages. They were reckless of their own lives. They poured themselves out.

> "They climbed the steep ascent of heaven,
> Through peril, toil and pain."

All the progress which the Church has made has been

made by such "reckless" Christians. To take just one modern instance, Father Heyer had that spirit when, the Kingdom of Christ needing help in India, although over seventy years of age, he was ready to go. From the worldly standpoint that was not very prudent. But it was greatly Christian. It was true to the spirit of Him who "became obedient unto death, even the death of the Cross." Nor will the Church come into the power that God stands ready to pour out upon it,—and through it salvation to mankind,—until our devotion and consecration become complete. The calculating, prudent discipleship which dilutes Christian loyalty, which refuses to make the final, abandoned "all out" reckless consecration of heart and mind and soul to Christ, will always be a limping discipleship.

Do you see, the Christian's "recklessness" is not real recklessness, at all? In the light of Eternal Destiny it is the only prudence. It is the longest-sighted wisdom. It is the wisdom of the man who, undertaking a project in which he believes with all his heart, will give everything he has to make it a success. The greatest cause of all, the salvation of eternal souls, is worth all the Christian can give to it. It only seems "reckless" to a world blinded by selfishness and low vision. A Christian stakes his life on the eternal values. He believes that God's will shall at last be done. He believes that a better world can be born, so that even in times like these he is lightened by that great Christian hope. Here he has faith to make life worth living, here he has a hope glorious enough to give a glow to life, and here he has a Christ who guarantees him victory. For the sake of that faith, to serve that hope, in the Name of that Christ, the Christian will give all!

MONDAY IN HOLY WEEK

Seeking to See Jesus

A. A. Hahn

MONDAY IN HOLY WEEK

AND there were certain Greeks among them that came up to worship at the feast: the same came therefore to Philip, which was of Bethsaida of Galilee, and desired him, saying, "Sir, we would see Jesus."

Philip cometh and telleth Andrew: and again Andrew and Philip tell Jesus.

And Jesus answered them, saying, "The hour is come, that the Son of man should be glorified.

"Verily, verily, I say unto you, except a corn of wheat fall into the ground and die, it abideth alone: but if it die, it bringeth forth much fruit. He that loveth his life shall lose it: and he that hateth his life in this world, shall keep it unto life eternal. If any man serve me, let him follow me; and where I am, there shall also my servant be: if any man serve me, him will my Father honour.

"Now is my soul troubled; and what shall I say? Father, save me from this hour: but for this cause came I unto this hour. Father, glorify thy name."

Then came there a voice from heaven, saying, "I have both glorified it, and will glorify it again."

The people therefore that stood by, and heard it, said that it thundered: others said, "An angel spake to him."

Jesus answered and said, "This voice came not because of me, but for your sakes. Now is the judgment of this world: now shall the prince of this world be cast out. And I, if I be lifted up from the earth, will draw all men unto me."

This he said, signifying what death he should die.

—John 12: 20-33

Seeking to See Jesus

SIR, we want to see Jesus!" This request was first made in recorded history by some Greeks. They brought the petition to Philip for an interview with the Master. Philip talked it over with Andrew (who had brought Peter to Jesus) and together they went to Jesus and told Him.

It seems like a simple request, yet it contains the desire, the longing, and the want of all mankind. Every man and woman sometime in his or her life feels this need for an interview with the Master. It may remain unexpressed and is often unrecognized even by the one who has this desire. But since the soul, the spirit of man which emanates from God cannot find rest until it returns to its element which is God, it must remain restless until it finds Jesus in whom we see God.

We all, like these Greeks of old, are hungry for the liberty of the children of God. We, too, have learned through bitter experience that the freedom for which we all crave is not the right to do what we choose, but rather the privilege to do what is right. We have learned that there are and must be certain laws governing freedom and that these laws must be obeyed. But we have tried so many laws and they all left us as empty and restless and bound as we were before.

So after all of our endeavors we finally cry out with the Greeks of our text: "Sir, we want to see Jesus."

And what is it that Jesus would tell them? He tells them that in order to enjoy the great harvest of their desire, they like wheat must first die. For, "Whosoever loves his life loses it, and whosoever hates his life in this world will preserve it for eternal life."

I would compare the individual person with a radio receiving set. How foolish to hate the receiver because of the terrible jungle noises or the inane soap operas that proceed from it. Such programs are really not enjoyed, they are but the rattle that is shaken in baby's face, causing baby to forget its discomfort for a brief time, but not removing the discomfort. I then notice, that all radios do not bring forth these same unsatisfying programs. I observe some that make the listener joyous, happy, peaceful and cause him to take new courage. And I say,—"Why is this?" Upon thoughtful and careful investigation I discover that these people are tuned in to a different station. And I, too, begin to twist dials and press buttons in the hope of finding that station. But by myself, without the dial reading, I cannot find it and I ask those who are tuned in,—"Sir, I would like you to tune me in on that station."—"Sir, we want to see Jesus."

I thought hatred was the proper law to follow, it would give me that satisfaction, that harvest of freedom I so desire. But I found the opposite. I found myself losing the few things I thought I possessed. Hating the radio receiver and smashing it brought me no joy. I found only those people free and enjoying themselves who having tuned in on Jesus, His thoughts, words and deeds, forgot themselves (the radio set) completely and thought only of the program they were permitted to send forth in *their* thoughts, words and deeds and how they might help others to do likewise. I found that when you lose your life for a cause, His cause, you could not hate anyone.

Then I tried fear and it enslaved me. No rest at any time and only disturbed sleep at night. It, too, made a slave of me. And I noticed him whose radio was tuned in on Jesus. He was like the paratrooper who steps fearlessly out into space, thousands of feet above the earth, knowing there is enough air all about him to open his chute and permit him to land safely. So the man who sees Jesus does not fear his enemies, he does not fear sickness, disaster or death. He knows that God who is with him and all about him is more powerful than all that could be against him. So utterly forgetful of self he walks boldly forth, knowing that God's love will open the chute of his endeavors and preserve him for eternal life. All things work together for good to those who love Him.

But I am so sensitive! What I actually mean is selfish. Sensitiveness is thinking of self. I must think of the other fellow. I must be in tune with the right station for his sake and help him to find this station also. If we would like the freedom which faith alone can give, we too must say with those Greeks, "Sir, we want to see Jesus." Yes, I tried selfishness and it made a miserable slave of me. Always asking, What will it do for *me,* mean to *me,* give *me?* And I found no peace with God or man.

Selfishness robbed me of peace with God, which I tried to find by being a good churchman, attending all services and paying all dues, but I did not find it. My righteousness was like that of the Scribes and Pharisees. And then I read of a man who, when lightning rods were first invented, took a piece of rod and tied it to the chimney of his house. The first thunderstorm that broke loose over his house struck it and completely demolished it. He thought lightning rods no good until a friend convinced him that electricity is not only in the sky but also in the earth, and that therefore the rod must be both imbedded in the earth and pointing to the sky. So by tuning in on Jesus I learned that in order to gain peace with God I must have peace with man. I must lose my life in the service to man while keeping my heart and mind tuned to God in heaven. Thus only can I gain the liberty of the children of God which comes through peace.

So in true repentance I must purge my soul of the poisons of hate, and fear and selfishness, tune them out; and fill my heart and mind with love and faith and peace, tune them in.

Today there are millions of people in America, in China, Japan, India, Africa and the Islands of the Sea who are crying to Andrew and Philip, you and me, "Sir, we would see Jesus." We are going to answer this prayer as did those disciples by letting His light so shine through us before men that they may see His good works of love, faith and peace; and by sending more and more missionaries to the sin-sick and hungry world, so that it, too, might forever tune out hatred and fear and selfishness and be filled instead with love, faith and peace so that the Son of Man may be glorified.

TUESDAY IN HOLY WEEK

Pride On Parade

Charles B. Foelsch

TUESDAY IN HOLY WEEK

THEN Jesus said unto them, "Yet a little while is the light with you. Walk while ye have the light, lest darkness come upon you: for he that walketh in darkness knoweth not whither he goeth. While ye have light, believe in the light, that ye may be the children of light." These things spake Jesus, and departed, and did hide himself from them.

But though he had done so many miracles before them, yet they believed not on him: that the saying of Esaias the prophet might be fulfilled, which he spake, "Lord, who hath believed our report? And to whom hath the arm of the Lord been revealed?"

Therefore they could not believe, because that Esaias said again, "He hath blinded their eyes, and hardened their heart; that they should not see with their eyes, nor understand with their heart, and be converted, and I should heal them." These things said Esaias, when he saw his glory, and spake of him.

Nevertheless among the chief rulers also many believed on him; but because of the Pharisees they did not confess him, lest they should be put out of the synagogue: for they loved the praise of men more than the praise of God.

Jesus cried and said, "He that believeth on me, believeth not on me, but on him that sent me. And he that seeth me seeth him that sent me. I am come a light into the world, that whosoever believeth on me should not abide in darkness. And if any man hear my words, and believe not, I judge him not: for I came not to judge the world, but to save the world. He that rejecteth me, and receiveth not my words, hath one that judgeth him: the word that I have spoken, the same shall judge him in the last day. For I have not spoken of myself; but the Father which sent me, he gave me a commandment, what I should say, and what I should speak. And I know that his commandment is life everlasting: whatsoever I speak therefore, even as the Father said unto me, so I speak." —*John 12: 35-50*

Pride On Parade

I AM FRANK to say this day's gospel puts a shudder in my soul, for it points a melancholy finger first at me, and you, and then at our demon-filled world. See what happens it seems to say when *The Parable of the Empty Soul* becomes a stark reality. See these people who ornamented their house of life with the little trinkets of religion, but left it empty of all real values, letting the demons slip in and take control, until at last their spirits are in blackness and their souls in clanking chains.

"Though he had done so many miracles before them, yet believed they not on him!"

It is a doleful picture,—The Tragedy of Love Refused. But Christ is in the picture, too, and so it cannot connote complete despair. He is life, and where there is life, there is hope!

The inspired writer makes plain to us here:

I. *How terrible that sin that makes men spurn their Christ!*

II. *How shameless the attitudes men strike when that sin comes to lodge with them.*

III. *How inexhaustible the love that despite its rejection refuses to let them go.*

I

How terrible that sin that makes men spurn their Christ!

If I were to put into the hand of each of you today a blank slip of paper with the request that you put down on it the deadliest sin you can think of, what sin would it be? Would you write down murder, sexual vice, drunkenness? Would your choice be war, or greed, or dishonesty?

Sober thinkers of all ages pass by these gross sins, every one, and unitedly put pride at the top of the list.

Now look upon life's stage and see the little Caesars and Napoleons and Hitlers strutting by, "fools in fermentation" as Butler puts it, "swelling and boiling over like a porridge pot"; and then in a moment going down to defeat and oblivion! Are you not ready to say "Amen" to the ancients' conviction that pride is the deadliest sin of them all?

Or, if you still wonder about it, look at your own soul's tendency to put self in the highest place, and to believe that God (whatever some people think of you) can hardly be blind to your basic inner excellence, and overlooking your tiny foibles and sins—after all He can't expect complete perfection!—must needs count your good deeds on the credit side of heaven's ledger! Which of us is free from this temptation? That is pride, and it is the worst sin of them all, because at the last it means to throw a man down to the bottom of the pit, and make him say, sullenly, even there, "I want no Jesus Christ to think that He could ever die for me!"

No wonder Scripture declares solemnly, "Pride goeth before destruction and a haughty spirit before a fall."

Please do not confuse pride with self-respect. That is quite a different quality, and there is such a thing as going too far with self-abasement. God does not want His children to grovel in the dust, or count themselves, with Dean Swift, "the meanest vermin that ever crawled on the face of the earth." With all his failures, man is God's best work on earth!

What a pity, though, that self-respect deteriorates so easily, becomes vanity, conceit, arrogance, insolence, scorn! Make a column of these, putting them down vertically, after the fashion of a problem in arithmetic, and add them up, and the sum total is that pride that goeth before destruction.

That was the sin that made these people of our gospel story spurn their Christ! They felt sure they did not need Him! They had their eyes on the glittering baubles of earth, until they developed spiritual cataracts, an opacity of the lens of the soul! No ray from the Sun of Righteousness could blaze its way through. Nay more, those bright beams only made their blindness worse, thickening the callouses (that's the root meaning of the word "hardening" in the fortieth verse) on the eyes of the soul, until those men were so blind that they blamed their misery on the insufficiency of Jesus Christ! "*Therefore* they could not believe! . . . They loved the praise of men . . ."

John Galsworthy in his "Country House" pictures the pride of people like that in the creed of the Pendyce family,

"I believe in my father and his father and his father's father, the makers and keepers of my estate, and I believe in myself and my son and my son's son. And I believe that we have made the country, and shall keep the country what it is. And I believe in the Public Schools, and especially the Public School that I was at. And I believe in my social equals and the country house, and in things as they are, forever and ever. Amen."[1]

---

[1] Publishers, Charles Scribner's Sons, New York.

Pride, the most grievous sin of them all, constantly seeks to fasten itself upon men, and these men had not learned lesson number one in the spiritual curriculum, "Humble yourselves under the mighty hand of God!" Therefore they went blind!

II

The fruits of blindness like that are always inevitable. We see plainly here:

The shameless attitudes men strike when this sin comes to lodge in their lives.

John draws the picture only in quick and sweeping outline here; he has painted a full-length portrait of pride on parade only a few chapters earlier. If you want to see men strut scornfully in Christ's presence, turn back to John's eighth chapter. It is a revolting picture, life size, and in the somber colors of sin's crimson and gloom's muddy grey.

"Then said the Jews . . ." It's hard, isn't it, as one reads on, to make sense of what they were saying? What sense indeed could one expect in the purple-faced angry outbursts of proud men, trapped by their own words, quite in the wrong, as they saw for themselves, with not a dog's chance of getting the better of the argument?

Men in that state break out with foolish, wicked words, and they did! "Why, you're crazy . . . you're just a foreigner, you're full of the devil . . . you're talking rubbish . . . listen, do you know who we are . . . we are no Samaritan dogs, ours is the best country in the world and we are the best people in it too . . . we are the children of Abraham, and you say, Before Abraham was I am . . . will you listen to the blasphemer, he's calling himself God; now we know he's got a devil!" Helpless rage and wounded pride goads them to insane fury, and they pick up rocks lying there, "Let's kill him; it's not fit that this blasphemer should live!"

No doubt they behaved shamefully this day also. The record does not say what they attempted against Christ, but it must have been wicked, for the story says, "These things spake Jesus, and departed, and did hide himself from them."

So it happened again, the thing that had happened a thousand times with endless variations in the story of God's eager seeking for man's best—man's pride got between him and his salvation; his pride blinded his eyes to his Saviour-God.

I think we all see now why even the ancients were sure that pride is the worst sin of them all. They knew that is what pride does. It shuts its eyes angrily to the winsome vision of God. It thrusts self into the center of the picture, arrogantly, and pushes God out. It even ascribes the words and deeds of Christ to the inspiration of the devil. It makes men twist and turn to get away from God, and stumbling, they go down into darkness, sightless as bats in the sunshine, exulting in their blindness!

We are not guilty, I know, of crude blasphemy like that! But we do still hold off our Lord with our spiritual self-sufficiency, with our half-way religious devotion, and with our reluctance to give up those sins that hide Him from us.

And I can see those luminous suffering eyes upon us, full of amazed wonder that we do not humble ourselves, and confess Him freely, proud to be His wherever we are. That, says the record, was the failure of the chief rulers. They believed on him after a fashion, but did not openly confess Him, "for they loved the praise of men more than the praise of God."

Often, our behavior, too, proves that we count, not Him, but the praise of men a chief good. So we sweat and strive in our pride to gather the goods of this world—"for a cap and bells our lives we pay"—going the limit to make ourselves comfortable and grand, keeping up with the Joneses and outdoing the Smiths, perhaps at Eastertime appearing in garb more resplendent than Solomon's ("nothing prouder than rustling in unpaid for silks!"). And Christ is there telling us that it's a terribly dangerous business for the soul, this business of thinking to make ourselves glorious with the shoddy goods of this world. It's pride that is at the bottom of it all, but we go right on with it, making a little gesture now and again of devotion to Him, and hardly batting an eye as we join in singing,

"Jesus I my cross have taken
All to leave and follow Thee . . ."

These "rulers of the people" in our gospel had had their high moment of vision, when there was an exultant song in the heart, because they were touched by the greatness of this Christ. But all that was now past, and so they struck an attitude, and strutted, and flung out fierce words at Christ, in their pride, and believed they were God's people!

III

Christ did not give them up to their threatening doom. *See how inexhaustible the Love that despite its rejection refuses to let them go!*

Ah, the gentleness of this Son of God, who had at His command the legions of angels, who might then and there have destroyed the mocking enemy one and all, might have dashed them in pieces like a potter's vessel. He merely "departed and hid himself from them." Forever? Not so, it was only for the moment; quickly He is back again to lay siege to their hearts with His one weapon, love, pleading, "I am come a light into the world, that whosoever believeth on me should not walk in darkness."

The quest of the Christ is a ceaseless quest,
 "I hid from him, and under running laughter. . . .
  From those strong feet that followed after,
      But with unhurrying chase
      And unperturbed pace,
  Deliberate speed, majestic instancy
      They beat, and a Voice beat
      More instant than the feet—"[1]

The unceasing quest of God . . . . to seek and to save! "Adam, where art thou?" is the loving, longing, seeking cry of God in the garden at the dawn of salvation's story. "O man, where art thou?" is God's cry through the ages, repeated wooingly, in the face of indifference and rejection, God never lapsing into silence, never growing weary.

The quest leads straight to Good Friday . . . and the Cross. "I died for you my children, and will ye treat me so?"

Marc Connelly's "Green Pastures" paints the picture, with

---

[1] Francis Thompson, "The Hound of Heaven."

strong strokes of pathos. God in high heaven looking down upon His people . . . what high hopes for them He has! But what a risk! Will they always reject His way? Terribly disturbed in His heart of hearts, He sends them a judge, and then a prophet, and then a priest, doing everything, anything, for them, as the noises of revelry and the shouts of earth's rebellion increase, never giving up, ever holding on!

At last, when the din of earth's deviltry is loudest comes Gabriel, with his trumpet. Surely it's come time to blow the blast of doom for a race that will not heed, will not have the gift of God's love, will not walk His way.

Gabriel speaks, "You look awful pensive, Lawd. You been sitten' yere, lookin' dis way, an awful long time. Is it somethin' serious, Lawd?" "Very serious, Gabriel."

And Gabriel, awed by His tone, speaks up, with his trumpet poised to sound the call of doom, "Lawd, is de time come for me to blow?" "Not yet, Gabriel."

God cannot give up; He must yet win rebellious man, win him with love, but ah, the cost . . . the suffering of it, appalling even to God . . . the Cross.

Then comes the Voice, from down on the earth, "Oh, look at him! Oh, look, dey goin' to make him carry it up dat high hill! Dey goin' to nail him to it!" . . . .[1]

"What does it mean this wood
So stained with blood,
This tree without a root

[1] Quotations from "The Green Pastures," by Marc Connelly, pub. Farrar & Rinehart, N. Y., 1929, copyright.

That bears such fruit,
This tree without a leaf
So leaved with grief?

"Though fool, I cannot miss
The meaning this.
My sin's stupendous price,
His sacrifice.
Where closest friendships end,
One friend, my Friend."

We need not trouble our souls overmuch as to what happened at last in the case of these men of our gospel who spurned their Christ that day long ago. If they came finally to complete spiritual ruin, it was only because to their last breath they persisted in their prideful rejection of the loving Christ. God forbid that it was so! Please God, let it not be so with us!

God is good. The Way is still open. The Cross still pleads. The Christ still calls. The feet still pursue.

"Halts by me that footfall:
Is my gloom, after all,
Shade of His hand, outstretched caressingly?
'Ah, fondest, blindest, weakest,
I am He whom thou seekest!
Thou dravest love from thee, who dravest me.' "[1]

[1] From "The Hound of Heaven"—Francis Thompson, copyright, John Lane Co. "Collected Works."

WEDNESDAY IN HOLY WEEK

Trafficking With The Enemy

Charles Leslie Venable

WEDNESDAY IN HOLY WEEK

NOW the feast of unleavened bread drew nigh, which is called the Passover. And the chief priests and scribes sought how they might kill him; for they feared the people.

Then entered Satan into Judas surnamed Iscariot, being of the number of the twelve. And he went his way, and communed with the chief priests and captains, how he might betray him unto them. And they were glad; and covenanted to give him money. And he promised, and sought opportunity to betray him unto them in the absence of the multitude.

—Luke 22: 1-6

Trafficking With The Enemy

Then entered Satan into Judas.—Luke 22: 3

IT IS important to keep our friendships in good repair. Life is constituted by its affinities. "A man's life consisteth not in the abundance of the things which he possesseth."[1] Religion is a matter of keeping our friendship with God and with all men in good repair. Irreligion is a matter of letting them fall into bad repair.

It is not less important to keep our enmities in good repair. There is a widespread notion that the New Testament calls upon us to eliminate all hate from our hearts. Nothing could be farther from the truth. Jesus said that we cannot love God and mammon. Human nature, He said, is so constituted that we must hate one and love the other; we must hold to the one and despise the other.[2] Far from commending any rose-water attitude of benevolent tolerance of everything, He condemns it. In the words of the seer of Patmos He says to the church at Laodicea, "Because thou art lukewarm, and neither cold nor hot, I will spue thee out of my mouth."[3] It is an illuminating

---

[1] Luke 12: 15.
[2] Matthew 6: 24.
[3] Revelation 3: 16.

thing to examine the New Testament to see how many times Jesus' anger broke out and His wrath overflowed. There are a great many more of them than we suspect. One day in the synagogue at Capernaum He called upon a man with a withered hand to stand up.[4] He asked the congregation whether He should heal him on the Sabbath day. Nobody answered a word. Then we are told that Jesus "looked round about on them with anger." One day He went into the temple in Jerusalem and seeing the merchandizing going on between men for the exploitation of the buyers and the corruption of the sellers, He made a whip of cords and drove out those that bought and sold and overturned the tables of the money changers, saying that God's house was to be a house of merchandise with God for the enrichment of all and the exploitation of none, the correction of all and the corruption of none.[5]

These two matters, hate and love, are two sides of one and the same thing. If there is anything wrong with one of them, the other is bound to be out of order too. It is a curious fact, but it is a significant one, that going to church made Jesus angry,—angry at the right things. It should do that for us too. That is to say that the place where we learn to love God and all men is the place where we ought no less to learn to hate everything that is against God and against our fellow men. It was because Jesus loved men, that His anger welled up at any acquiescence, under any pretext whatever, of anything that laid a handicap even on the hand of a man. When Jesus drove the traders out of the temple, St. John tells us that "his disciples

---

[4] Mark 3: 1-5.
[5] John 2: 13-17.

remembered that it was written, 'The zeal of thine house hath eaten me up.' "[6]

Such zeal for God's house can only be achieved and sustained over against an equal enmity for those things which contaminate and corrupt, desecrate and defeat God's house in the work which it is to do in the world. This is the thing modern psychology has been saying for a long time. Our strength of character, it has been saying, is in our sentiments. These sentiments are not a simple affection for some one or some thing. They are complex emotional systems consisting of loves and hates, faiths and fears. Complexes, the term used to represent mental and moral disturbances, are emotional systems in which these loves and hates, fears and faiths have gotten out of focus and fastened themselves on to the wrong things. It is only such an emotional system as is represented by a sentiment which is capable of releasing and enlisting that instinctive energy which we call will power. The absence of any such strong sentiments is the source of boredom and of impotence. "Man is only truly great," said Benjamin Disraeli, "when he acts from his passions." Unfortunately, man is only base then, too. The truth is that he is only truly great when his passions are in the control of great sentiments which not only can enlist them but also can control them, sentiments which keep the passions both in good repair and in the right focus.

It is important to keep our hates in good repair, also, because there is reason to believe that this is the side of character which emerges first. The living organism when it comes into

[6] John 2: 17.

the world has such desperate need for defense if it is to survive that it has to be armed with all kinds of resistance against its foes. "Most children," says Jespersen,[7] "learn to say 'no' before they learn to say 'yes'—simply because negation is a stronger expression of feeling than affirmation." Those people who are most skillful in manipulating and managing people know this. They know that man's hates and fears lie closest to the surface. They direct their appeals to them and they succeed in fusing men, thereby, into some of the most remarkable actions we ever see. It would be strange if Jesus who knew men best had not known this. But He did. He said, "Fear not them which kill the body, but are not able to kill the soul: but rather fear him which is able to destroy both soul and body in hell."[8] He has commanded us, not to eliminate our hates and fears, but to keep them in good repair and to keep them in the right focus.

This is the baseness which is involved in all betrayal. When we cease to hate the things that we ought to hate as we ought to hate them, then we cease to love ourselves and others as we ought to love them. When that happens we begin to traffic with the enemy and we awake to find that we have betrayed ourselves and those whom we ought to love as ourselves.[9] It was when Judas ceased to hate the things he ought to have hated as he ought to have hated them that he began negotiations with the chief priests and captains. Not that he should

---

[7] Otto Jespersen: Language, Its Nature, Development and Origin. Henry Holt and Co. 1924. p. 136.

[8] Matthew 10: 28.

[9] Matthew 22: 39.

have hated them. We are, indeed, told to love all men.[10] But he should have hated everything they represented. He should have so hated their conniving that he could never have connived. He should have so hated their corruption that he could never have been corrupted. It was when his hatred got out of focus and got out of repair that Satan entered into him.

To be sure such a collapse never comes in a moment. We are told with certainty two things about Judas. In the first place, he was taking money from the common purse, the group treasury, with which he was entrusted.[11] We are certainly near the beginning of his downfall here. He had no hate for the lust for money such as Jesus had. He had never looked around and seen the hateful, hideous thing the love of money is, in its corruption of the rich and its oppression of the poor. Because he had no adequate hate where he ought to have had a hate, he began to traffic with the enemy. Because he had no adequate hate for the love of money, he had no adequate love for the life of those whose lives are free and full because their wants are few and all fulfilled by the goodness of God. He didn't thrill to the blessedness of the poor.[12] Because he didn't hate the one, he didn't love the other. Because he had no strong guard of hate at the gate of his soul, Satan entered into him.

In the second place, Judas thought of himself as clever. It is probable that Judas never expected to betray Jesus; that he merely thought that if he could bring things to a head by getting Jesus arrested, Jesus would have to assert His powers or

10 Romans 12: 14.
11 John 12: 6.
12 Matthew 5: 3; Luke 6: 20.

His followers would be so aroused that they would overthrow those in power and establish Jesus' rule on earth. Judas' subsequent remorse and suicide when things didn't turn out that way almost make necessary such a reading of the events. If this be right it only confirms the fact that Judas thought of himself as clever. This business of singing a hymn and going out into the garden to pray, this business of telling parables about God's love and telling people to love each other only disgusted him.

Every criminal thinks that he is smarter than other people. The one thing that dominates his poor twisted mind is contempt for the "dumb clucks" who swallow the stuff about truth, love and justice. The one fundamental thing that his poor addled brain rejects is the idea of equality and humility among men. There is abundant evidence that Judas often irritated and aggravated his fellow disciples with this attitude of contempt and this assumption of superiority. Because he didn't hate contempt for one's fellow man as Jesus did and because he didn't hate attitudes of inequality as Jesus did, Judas did not love men and he didn't love humility as Jesus did. Because he didn't hate the one he should have hated, he hated the one he should have loved. Because he didn't set a strong guard of hate at the door of his soul, Satan entered into him.

Are we building up in ourselves strong enough hates; that is, hates against the right things? Are we keeping our hates in the right focus and in good repair? Someone has said that the reason twelve- to sixteen-year-old boys and girls are lost to the church in such large numbers at that period in their lives is because we have not built any adequate church sentiment into their lives. Might it be that we have done a fairly good job in teaching them why they should go to church, on which most men seem to agree, but that we have not built any adequate hate against the sloth, indifference and hypocrisy which prevents us from keeping our friendship with God, which we profess, in any decent or functioning order? Many men tell us with breath-taking frankness that they hate the tedium of church going, but they are not bothered about desertion or betrayal to God! That is all Judas did. He didn't hate the things he ought to have hated, so he hated the things he ought to have loved. He did not set a strong guard of hate as a sentinel at the door of his soul, so Satan entered into him.

Anyone can extend the list indefinitely. The boy or girl who doesn't have a strong enough hatred for the habit-forming, home-breaking, mind-debasing work of alcohol, is simply not equipped for life. Let no one say that we can't so paint things black or white; that one man's poison is another man's food; that one man may drink his alcohol like a gentleman while another man practices his abstinence like a Pharisee. To be sure you can't draw such a line between men, condemning a man because he uses alcohol or sanctifying another because he doesn't. But concerning alcohol there is such line to be drawn. Its habit-forming nature is to be feared and hated. All the rest is trafficking with the enemy, loving what we ought to hate and hating what we ought to love.

Anyone who doesn't have an adequate hatred for race discrimination, is certainly trafficking with the enemy in these times and preparing to play the part of a traitor in our day. If we don't hate race discrimination enough, we will not love one another enough to have a unified world. If we don't all rise together to a hatred of race discrimination, we are all going to fall together in a hatred of one another. When we don't hate the things we ought to hate, then we come to hate the things we ought to love, in this case, our fellow children of God, our Father. If we don't set the sentinel of a strong enough hate at the door of our souls, then Satan will enter into us, and we will betray both ourselves and those we ought to love as ourselves.

It is obvious that at the end of the war, the world is going to have a great quantity of hate on hand. That has always been the case at the end of every war and there is every indication that this war is going to excel all other wars in that also. This hate has always spilled over into crime, into race riots, and into civil and industrial strife. Our government is already planning how it will repossess for private and civil use the vast quantities of war materials which we expect to have on hand at the end of the war. Ought not the church to be thinking about what to do with the vast body of hate which will be on hand when the war ends? One has reason to believe that if the church tries to repress this hate by sitting on it to hold it down the church will only get blown to pieces for its pains and the world with it. All the time, the church could use all of this hate if we were just intelligent enough to repossess it and use it in the right directions. There is sound psychological and sociological reason for believing that if we don't, there is nothing that can keep Satan from entering in and the kingdoms of this world becoming the kingdom of sin.

THURSDAY IN HOLY WEEK

The Miracle of Grace

Emil E. Fischer

THURSDAY IN HOLY WEEK

AND when the hour was come, he sat down, and the twelve apostles with him. And he said unto them, "With desire I have desired to eat this passover with you before I suffer: for I say unto you, I will not any more eat thereof, until it be fulfilled in the kingdom of God."

And he took the cup, and gave thanks, and said, "Take this, and divide it among yourselves: for I say unto you, I will not drink of the fruit of the vine, until the kingdom of God shall come."

And he took bread, and gave thanks, and brake it, and gave unto them, saying, "This is my body, which is given for you: this do in remembrance of me."

Likewise, also the cup after supper, saying, "This cup is the new testament in my blood, which is shed for you."

—*Luke 22: 14-20*

The Miracle of Grace

And he took bread, and gave thanks, and brake it, and gave unto them, saying, This is my body which is given for you: this do in remembrance of me. Likewise also the cup after supper, saying, This cup is the new testament in my blood, which is shed for you.
—Luke 22: 19, 20

THIS is the day, in the Church's year, made memorable by the institution of the Lord's Supper. It was the same night in which He was to be betrayed. Judas had completed his bargain with the chief priests and rulers of the people. In a few hours he would betray his Master. Jesus would be apprehended and His lonely march to Calvary would be begun. But the remaining hours Jesus had planned to devote to His disciples. He did not want them to remain comfortless; and so He told them about the Comforter whom He would send, the Spirit of truth and power, who would guide them into all truth, endue them with power to be His witnesses, and ultimately lead them to the place where their Master was about to go to prepare for their own coming. "Let not your heart be troubled," He admonishes them, "ye believe in God, believe also in me." Whatever the morrow might bring forth for their Master, or their own experience have in store for them, they were to have the assurance that their trust and confidence in

Jesus had not been misplaced. They were to believe in Him, and by believing in Him attain to victory, even over death.

But it was not only by the promise of the Holy Spirit, the Comforter, that Jesus sought to prepare His disciples for what lay before them. There was another way in which He willed to accomplish His purpose. He gave them the promise of His own presence, and that in a most unique way. "And he took bread," we read, "and gave thanks, and brake it, and gave it unto them, saying, This is my body which is given for you: this do in remembrance of me. Likewise also the cup after supper, saying, This cup is the new testament in my blood, which is shed for you."

The words and action are familiar to us. We repeat them as often as we gather to celebrate the Lord's Supper. Seen against the background of that solemn scene in the upper room, their meaning becomes plain. When Jesus first spoke the words and communicated the bread and wine to His disciples, He was still with them in body. And He promises that He will be with them again in a similar way when all will be fulfilled and He would sit down and sup with them in the completed Kingdom of God. But what of the years that lay between? On the morrow Jesus knew that He would be crucified and His disciples scattered. He would indeed arise again the third day and appear unto His disciples. But they would be in need of more than simply the assurance that He was alive. They would want some pledge that the fruits of His life and death were not lost to them. And it is against that attitude of mind that Jesus did what He did. In the gift of His body and blood He gave Himself, with all that He was and all that He did, together with the promise that as often as they did this in remembrance of Him, He would be present to impart Himself to them as their Lord and Savior.

This is what the Sacrament has continued to mean down through the ages. Whenever and wherever men have gathered and done this in remembrance of Him they have been conscious of a communion with the crucified and risen Lord. To us that communion has always meant a communion with a Real Presence. As truly as Jesus was present in body with His disciples at that first communion, so truly is He present with us when He imparts Himself to us with the bread and wine of the Eucharist. That is a miracle of grace. Understand it with the mind we cannot, for its meaning lies hidden in the depths of the wisdom and knowledge of God. It is God's gift, bestowed out of His unsearchable love for the children of men, and must be received in faith. This, however, is our assurance. Christ has promised; His word cannot be broken. "This is my body. . . . This is the cup of the new testament in my blood." That word promises His presence, and we believe His word.

What this communion with Christ has meant in the way of blessing will be revealed only when the secrets of the human heart are laid bare. Each of us brings to the altar his own peculiar need to find it satisfied there by the manifold grace of our Lord Jesus Christ. But there are great elemental blessings in which all share alike and which become the inexhaustible source of comfort and strength.

One of these is the assurance that the redeeming love with which God so loved the world that He gave His only-begotten Son for its redemption is bestowed upon me individually and alone. We need to know that. God's love is an intensely personal love, and until I have experienced it as such I have not learned to know its comforting and sustaining power. It is when I am overwhelmed with the thought of my aloneness that I need to lay hold on the love of God for *me.* It is when my sin rises before me to accuse me that I need to hear God speak to *me,* Thy sins are forgiven thee. Others, too, may be racked by pain upon beds of illness, but God must speak to me to give *me* strength to bear. There is none without his burden of sorrow, disappointment or despair, but God must speak to me to lift the burden which rests on *me.* And this He does when I hear the words, Take and eat, this is the Body of Christ given for thee. Take and drink, this is the Blood of the New Testament shed for thy sins. It is God's gift to *me;* the pledge and seal that His redeeming love has been made to rest upon me.

But the assurance that God's love goes out to me is made possible only because it is a forgiving love and clothes me with a righteousness which is not my own but is reckoned to my account for Christ's sake. That is the great truth without which there could be no real communion with God. There is a communion among men created naturally by common interests, common tasks, or common gifts and talents. But who are we to claim the right to have communion with God? God is holy and I am unholy. God is righteous and I am unrighteous. God is God and I am a poor, weak, sinning mortal. Yet, even so, God invites me to have communion with Him. "For thus saith the high and lofty One that inhabiteth eternity, whose name is Holy; I dwell in the high and holy place, with him also that is of a contrite and humble spirit." (Isaiah 57: 15.) It is all for Christ's sake, the Christ who loved me and gave Himself for me. And in the Lord's Supper I become assured of it, for it is there that I receive His broken body and shed blood for the remission of my sin. I depart from the Communion Table with the conviction renewed and strengthened in me that I am a son of God. God is my Father; I am His child, with all that that implies so far as intimate personal communion with Him is concerned.

That very fact, that in the Lord's Supper our sonship is certified, carries with it another aspect of communion. There is a communion with one another created by our common communion with God through Christ. Sons of God are brothers to one another. In the Lord's Supper our brotherhood in Christ is renewed and strengthened. The divine forgiveness in which we share becomes a power to constrain us to a like forgiveness of our fellow men, however unworthy they may seem to be. The divine compassion becomes a power to constrain us to a like compassion toward those who need the help that we can give. The divine sacrifice becomes a power to constrain us to a like devotion whereby we are willing to spend and be spent in sacrificial service for others. Forgiveness and brotherly kindness, service and sacrifice—these are the marks of Christian brotherhood, and in the Lord's Supper they are put upon us through our faith in the Christ who imparts Himself to us. Thus the communion of saints, created by faith, becomes a brotherhood of Christian service, in which the fruits of Christ's suffering and death on the Cross are made to appear in a newness of life, for the healing of our estrangements.

These are the gifts with which we depart from the Lord's Table. In the Sacrament provision has been made in a unique way for the impartation of the grace of God as it is found in Jesus Christ. To be sure, that grace is also present in the Word that is preached. But in the Sacrament it comes to us with a peculiar simplicity and inclusiveness. There the spoken word is re-enforced with a divinely ordained action, and the Christ becomes ours, with all His gifts and benefits, as we receive the earthly elements with which the words are joined. Only one thing is necessary and that is faith;—not that faith creates the gift which God desires to bestow: the gift is there by God's own miracle of grace. But faith alone can enable us to receive the gift worthily and to our salvation.

May God therefore grant unto us as we come to the Sacrament of the Lord's Supper that we may come with penitent and believing hearts, hungering and thirsting for the righteousness with which it clothes us before God. And may we depart from the altar with joyful hearts, full of gratitude for the blessings of our sonship, renewed and increased in us through the Christ who has imparted Himself to us.

GOOD FRIDAY

Life's Eternal Plus

Oscar F. Blackwelder

GOOD FRIDAY

AND there followed him a great company of people, and of women, which also bewailed and lamented him. But Jesus turning unto them, said, "Daughters of Jerusalem, weep not for me, but weep for yourselves, and for your children. For, behold, the days are coming, in the which they shall say, Blessed are the barren, and the wombs that never bare, and the paps which never gave suck. Then shall they begin to say to the mountains, Fall on us; and to the hills, Cover us. For if they do these things in a green tree, what shall be done in the dry?"

And there were also two other, malefactors, led with him to be put to death. And when they were come to the place, which is called Calvary, there they crucified him, and the malefactors, one on the right hand, and the other on the left.

Then said Jesus, "Father, forgive them; for they know not what they do." And they parted his raiment and cast lots.

And the people stood beholding. And the rulers also with them derided him, saying, "He saved others; let him save himself, if he be Christ, the chosen of God."

And the soldiers also mocked him coming to him, and offering him vinegar, and saying, "If thou be the king of the Jews, save thyself." And a superscription also was written over him, in letters of Greek, and Latin, and Hebrew, THIS IS THE KING OF THE JEWS.

And one of the malefactors which were hanged railed on him, saying, "If thou be Christ, save thyself and us."

But the other answering, rebuked him, saying, "Dost not thou fear God, seeing thou art in the same condemnation? And we indeed justly; for we receive the due reward of our deeds: but this man hath done nothing amiss."

And he said unto Jesus, "Lord, remember me when thou comest into thy kingdom."

And Jesus said unto him, "Verily I say unto thee, To day shalt thou be with me in paradise."

And it was about the sixth hour, and there was a darkness over all the earth until the ninth hour. And the sun was darkened, and the veil of the temple was rent in the midst.

And when Jesus had cried with a loud voice, he said, "Father, into thy hands I commend my spirit:" and having said thus, he gave up the ghost.

—Luke 23: 27-46

Life's Eternal Plus

"JESUS plowed Himself into human history and His Cross was the point of the plow." So the Cross is the key to Jesus, as Jesus is the key to the life of God. How we do need that key today! Indeed, a religion or philosophy of life with no cross or a small cross in it can never save, interpret, or heal a world filled with crosses. The Divine Tragedy is at home in a world of human tragedy. Good Friday, as the Day of the Cross, therefore, makes Him at home in our world and places Him in our history. "He suffered under Pontius Pilate." That dates Him in our human records as He was already "slain from the foundation of the world."

In the first paragraph of the Gospel for today there is sharp warning against building a sense of pity about the Cross. Jesus doesn't want to be pitied. He doesn't ask for tears of sympathy. He wants to be trusted. He knew what He was doing. They didn't take His life, He gave it. Why pity Him for doing that? He couldn't have been more specific than when He said, "Weep not for me but for yourselves." It is easy so to present the Cross that we awaken only sentiment for the physical suffering of Christ, but that is not really preaching the Cross.

Not only is there the warning against false sympathy—there is also in the Gospel for Good Friday a glimpse of deep social significance. Don't forget that Jesus was crucified between two thieves who, by the confession of at least one of them, were getting what they deserved. Thus the ancient word was coming true, "He was numbered with the transgressors." Really, wouldn't it be hard to think of Jesus dying alone? There would seem a selfishness about it. He who craved companionship in Gethsemane had it on Calvary. He had said, I am *among you* as he that serveth" and He was *among* men to the end. He identified Himself all the way with men just as they were. "He ate with publicans and sinners," and now He was dying with them. It looks like part of His Incarnation. His critics out front on the Day of the Cross didn't see that this identification was a necessary step in saving men. Not even you and I can do much for people and save ourselves at the same time. Jesus saved others by losing Himself.

Having talked as they did, you wonder why the folks out front wanted His robe. Why did they go to the trouble of gambling for it? And, if they had Him correctly classified between two thieves, why, unless for sarcasm, did they put the sign over His head, "THIS IS THE KING OF THE JEWS"? The whole scene seems to fit the title, "That Strange Man Hanging on a Cross." However, for many of us "That Strange Man" has become a Living Presence. We have learned that though there were three crosses on Calvary, the one in the middle was different—"It was luminous with God." That Cross for us makes all the difference in a world filled with crosses. We know now, among other assurances, that God suffers when we suffer.

You see life soon brings every normal person to some kind of a cross. If you have no crosses, look out, you may be missing life altogether. So Calvary, which is the epitome of the whole human story, had three kinds of crosses. There was the cross of the critical thief. There was the cross of the praying thief. And there was the Middle Cross, lighted with God, which made the difference between the crosses on either side. It's either cynicism or prayer always—and that Middle Cross still turns the first into the second. In this way, at least, His Cross is the key to life.

And here is a word about putting off this "turning." Calvary shows the possibility of deathbed repentance. That is what the praying thief means. But if he shows the possibility of deathbed repentance, the other thief shows the improbability. The difficulty is not that Christ cannot hear but that we cannot speak; not that He may become deaf, but that we may become dumb. Cynicism has its way.

I was just saying that Calvary epitomizes the whole human story. Around His Cross every type of person seems to have had a representative. Humanity was there. The thieves were present under arms but the rest of the crowd were drawn by some other strange power. And, for many of them it was more than nauseating curiosity. It looks like they had part in the scene. Consider the points of view they represented.

Of course, *Mary* was there for very personal reasons but she represents motherhood across the generations and the way of life for motherhood speaks in this wise: Risk your life on a possible tragedy for something worth risking it for and get a destiny out of it. . . . We have already talked about the *two thieves*—their way of life read: Put into life as little as you can and take out as much as you can. That always leads to a cross, perhaps imprisonment, and surly remorse. . . . And there were the *disciples,* timid and fearful, but they seem to symbolize those who hear His personal Word from the Cross in every generation: I give you that quality of life with which disease, death, and poverty have nothing to do. . . . And the *centurion* in charge of the crucifixion was there. He had to see the thing through. By following the sworn path of duty he came to the conviction that would not let him go, "Certainly this was a righteous man." . . . And the *people* were there, victims then as now of political trickery and illustrating the fickleness of humanity. From "Hosannahs" to "Crucify him" in one week—who said "the voice of the people is the voice of God?" . . . And *Simon of Cyrene* was there. That man gets me. He bore Christ's Cross after Him and must have seen expressions in His face that others farther away missed. He perhaps heard groans and sighs and whispers reserved then and now for those who bear His Cross after Him. . . . I wonder where and how *Nicodemus* and *Joseph of Arimathea* spent the day before they went to claim the body from Pilate. . . . And I wonder if *Pilate's wife* was somewhere near by, perhaps in hiding, but where she could glimpse at least at a distance This Strange Man who haunted her dreams. . . . And, put this down, *Annas* got around to see if He was really dead. . . . And, count on this, *Caiaphas* and *Herod* got around, also. . . . And I'm very sure that *Barabbas* was near by, saying to himself, "He died for me." . . . Complete the list of the "dramatis personae of the Divine Tragedy" for yourself. But, don't forget, *you* and *I* were there, too.

Having looked at the personnel around the Cross, let us now look more intently at the Figure on that central Cross.

Trying to interpret what He is doing there is the greatest business of preaching.

If His Cross were only the story of a man, hanging on a crossbeam of wood, giving his life for what he deeply believed, any good newspaper reporter could tell that story in a few paragraphs. However, the finest of Christian scholarship, the best of Christian experience and the truest of Christian insight for twenty centuries have not been able to fathom the depths of the Cross. In an effort to do so great scholars and saints of the Church have developed at least five theories of what Jesus did on His Cross. There is mighty truth in each of them and material to illustrate or substantiate each of them is found in this Gospel.

First, there is the *Ransom Theory.* Jesus gave "His life a ransom for many." Never mind to whom the ransom was paid, the real question is whether we for whom He died are still of sin the slaves? Are we free men?

There is no doubt that He set the praying, penitent thief free. The thief only asked to be "remembered" but Jesus gave him more than he asked for. Jesus assured the poor fellow that he would be "with him." To know Christ's living presence, His resources, guidance and companionship under any and all circumstances, anywhere and everywhere—that is the greatest, if not the only, security and freedom this earth knows. Standing fast in the liberty wherewith Christ has set us free means to get from this living presence of Jesus the power to do what we ought to do. Freedom is not the right to do what one pleases—that pretty generally means slavery of some kind. Freedom, on the other hand, means achievement. Away, then, with old habits that enslave! Away with the demand for selfish rights. Let's talk the language of freedom which means obligations and responsibilities. What good is freedom of speech if we have nothing to say? What good is freedom of worship if we have no God to worship? And what worth is economic security if we don't know what to do with our security? A free man is one who is ready to be and capable of being the free instrument of the Eternal—the mind, the heart, the life through which Christ can think, love and act. That means to possess His living presence. "Today shalt thou be with me." To be thus set free is to be "ransomed" indeed.

Second, there is the *Governmental Theory.* Interesting that this conception should have been propounded by the founder of international law! Nothing so interferes with the government and life of men as the presence of evil in personal life and social relationships. And no other person in human history has handled this power of evil as has Jesus. It is His greatest gift to men. He is the first of earth's great not alone because of His own personal perfection but because of what He can do to handle the power and presence of evil in every man's life. But, take His Cross away from Him, and this gift of handling sin is weakened if not removed. The Cross is His instrument. Indeed, He rules from the Cross. The Cross literally decreases the amount of evil in the world and makes human government of men more possible. The obvious need for this in our day is writ large across the face of the whole earth.

You and I are so constructed that we may take in the streams of hate now flowing through the hearts of men, guide these streams into the hands of Christ where He will destroy them forever. To work with Him in the conquering and destruction of evil is the work of men of God. When Jesus prayed on the Cross, "Father, forgive them," He wasn't painting daffodils on a canvas or whistling in the dark or day dreaming. He was talking the only realism this earth knows. Indeed, the only way to get along with races, classes and conflicting national traditions and interests is "appreciation," which stems from "forgiveness." The very genius of human government is here. Government exists not by force—of course, that is necessary in dealing with some minorities and the state does possess the right of force by divine institution—but lasting government exists by the "consent of the governed." Consent means mutual confidence and good will. So while the world needs economic engineers and social planners, beneath and beyond both of these, society needs builders of good will to make the engineers and planners possible. This good will is the echo of the Angels' Song over Bethlehem and the Cross of Christ makes the song of the angels come true. Here is the Governmental Theory of the Cross. Christ rules from the wood for there He handles the basic problem of human sin and evil.

Third, there is the *Moral Influence Theory.* The Cross speaks in words like these: Look what love will do for what it believes and for whom it loves. So the Cross calls men to enlarge their "beliefs" and "loves." Remember what Jesus said on that Cross and consider the moral influence of His example. . . . "Father, forgive them": what a moral influence and ideal that is! "Woman, behold thy son . . . behold thy mother!"—Seeing one's family obligations through—what a moral ideal that is! "I thirst": There is no spiritual value in drinking a cup of water alone but to share it with a thirsty, needy brother is a spiritual experience, for it may mean doing it unto Him who thirsted on the Cross—what a moral ideal that is! "It is finished"—Seeing life through to a glorious finish, completing a task without stopping in the middle—what a moral ideal that is! Who can ever estimate the sacrificial living the Cross has inspired? Nothing short of a Christ who set the example of suffering as the Christian way of dealing with human problems would inspire men to suffer for what they believe. Jesus would never have inspired a Kagawa without His Cross. Nor a David Livingstone. Nor a Wilfred Grenfell. Nor an Abraham Lincoln.

Some evangelical Christians seem to be afraid of this approach to the Cross while some "liberals" stand here alone and go no further. But this theory is immortal. The Cross dare not be separated from the good life. It is from the Cross that the dynamic of Christian ethics comes. This is the Moral Influence Theory of the Cross. From that Cross comes the power to carry on in the good life.

Fourth, there is the *Subtitutionary Theory.* His critics out front on the Day of the Cross cried, "If thou be the king of the Jews, save thyself." But Jesus couldn't save Himself and us.

To make this matter crystal clear, let's try to put ourselves into the shoes or sandals of one man who will never forget that day. That man is Barabbas. He was the man previously condemned to die but the people elected Jesus to the Cross in His place. Indeed, God Himself had appointed Jesus. Some cruel, brutal, seemingly unfair things that men do seem to be under the control of a mighty move of the Eternal like the tide of the sea.

Surely Barabbas was standing there, near the Cross, constantly saying to himself, "He died for me. . . . He is taking my place." That is the way every penitent heart must feel. Jesus set Barabbas free by taking his place. He sets us free by taking ours.

"There was no other good enough
To pay the price of sin;
He only could unlock the gate
Of heaven, and let us in."

Fifth, there is the *Reconciliation Theory.* "God was in Christ, reconciling the world unto himself." Men everywhere were prodigals. They had wandered far from the Father's heart and purpose. Sin had come between them and His fellowship.

So Jesus announced, "And I, if I be lifted up from the earth will draw all men unto me." The Cross was the magnet by which God drew men back to His fellowship and purpose. And now, let's change the tense. It is not past but present. Jesus draws men to Himself through the pulling power of the Cross and so reconciles men and God. God never needed to be reconciled. He loves men forever. Man is the prodigal and the Cross draws him back to the Father's heart.

There are at least two facts in the heart of God: His world and His Son. "God so loved the world that he gave his Son." To bring these two together is the mission of the Cross.

When the prodigal came home in Jesus' classic parable and when prodigals still come home in the dust of everyday life, at least three experiences are theirs. It is said that the ring the father of the prodigal put on his son's finger, stood for love;

the shoes meant freedom since slaves went barefooted; the new robe for his shoulders stood for protection. To be "reconciled" to God means to be sure of His forgiving love, His freedom, His protection. It means to be on family terms with God. It means to be "at-one-ment" with the Eternal. What more can we say? What more can the human heart desire?

Have you heard about the small boy who went with his father to visit a great Cathedral? As they walked under the giant arches, the boy asked, "Daddy, what is the big plus sign up front?" Of course, he was referring to the cross on the high altar. That is just what the Cross is—life's eternal plus. What you are now plus this Cross of Christ equals the man you ought to be—that is the Gospel. Jesus erects His eternal plus beside your life and mine and asks, "What do ye more than others?" The Cross is not alone the key to life—it is *Life's Eternal Plus.*

GOOD FRIDAY

The Seven Words From the Cross

Theodore K. Finck

GOOD FRIDAY

The First Word:

Father, forgive them; for they know not what they do. *—Luke 23: 34*

The Second Word:

Verily I say unto thee, To day shalt thou be with me in paradise. *—Luke 23: 43*

The Third Word:

Woman, behold thy son!—Behold thy mother. *—John 19: 26, 27*

The Fourth Word:

My God, my God, why hast thou forsaken me? *—Matthew 27: 46*

The Fifth Word:

I thirst. *—John 19: 28*

The Sixth Word:

It is finished. *—John 19: 30*

The Seventh Word:

Father, into thy hands I commend my spirit *—Luke 23: 46*

The Seven Words from the Cross

AS we gather about the cross of Jesus for three hours on Good Friday, we hear the Master's voice in seven separate utterances. These great "Words," as they are called, weave a pattern for us, which at one and the same time illumines the Saviour's physical dying and portrays vital principles of His redemptive ministry.

Studying the pattern, we find first of all that three Words occur early in the crucifixion. They are the Master's last will and testament to those near by—His enemies, his fellow sufferer on another cross, His mother.

Then the human life of the Son of God ebbs. He sinks rapidly in spirit and in body. The Fourth and Fifth Words are heard from the valley of the shadow of His death. The darkness which was over all the land was no thicker than the darkness which separated the Crucified One from God.

At last the pattern reveals death, but triumph has returned. The last two Words are the Saviour's own verdict on it all—the Sixth Word taking a postview, the Seventh Word a preview. With this last Word the Resurrection has almost begun.

May Jesus, now alive forevermore, be with us as we meditate on the Sayings from the Cross. May He include us in the audience of those who hear His Seven Words—words of forgiveness, blessing, and reassurance.

Above all may we not, while we are practicing the fellowship of His sufferings by our worship, be crucifying Him afresh by our lives.

THE FIRST WORD

Father, forgive them; for they know not what they do.—Luke 23: 34

MEN," said Piney, "tonight we cut the trunk wire!"

"You mean, Piney"—the men crowded about him were aghast—"you mean the wire that carries the current into Clarkstown?"

"Yes." Piney was firm. "The Electric Company won't budge. So we're going to show them we mean business. Tonight, then!"

In Clarkstown was Piney's home. Shortly after he had left it that afternoon his little daughter—idol of his heart—had fallen violently ill. The doctor came. Dusk fell while the physician was examining the child.

"Give me the brightest light you can," he said tensely. "I must operate—at once."

The largest bulb in the house beamed brightly for the physician as he worked long over his patient. "Now, if this one last step goes well—"

Out, the lights! The whole house, the whole town, was dark.

"Quick, light!" shrieked the physician. "Turn on the light!

She's dying! Thirty seconds more . . . light! light! . . . Too late! She's gone." . . .

"Father, forgive them, *for they know not what they do.*"

Can it be that we, like Piney in the story, like the soldiers beneath the Cross, are doing violent deeds of whose real results we are in ignorance?

The Crucified One must have been thinking of many people when the First Word was spoken from the Cross: of the apostles, who deserted Him; of the priests, who hated Him; of the mobsters, who yelled for His life; of Pilate, who mishandled justice; of the soldiers, who were harsh with His helpless person. One and all, Jesus felt, did what they did because they did not understand, did not realize.

What did they not realize?

This, that by their actions they were killing the Divine One, and working against God and His Kingdom and righteousness.

Jesus magnanimously prayed God to forgive them. Freely he released them from any anger on His part. "Whosoever speaketh a word against the Son of Man, it shall be forgiven him," He might have said for the second time.

But may there have been a further reason why Jesus said, "*Father,* forgive them?" The criminal's case the Saviour handled directly: "Today shalt thou be with me." This case was referred to God.

The underlying truth seems to be that when a man or nation "realizes," and repents—appraises the wrong and turns toward the Redeemer—good can be expected to result. The fruit is morally certain. But when a man or nation continues sinning unknowingly, not stopping to calculate the real evil, not repenting, the Redeemer is not in position to help. The only chance then is that God can somehow overrule the error. The Father, by means of His providence, may be able to "forgive."

We hope that some good comes out of the Second World War. Since men and nations have not been able to control the situation in a Christlike way, any such good can come only because the Almighty has superseded the wrath of man. Certainly men knew not what they did.

Joseph Fort Newton once asserted in a sermon—and pled the point most searchingly—that the stupidity of man causes as much suffering as his sin. If we accept the distinction, the *sinful* evildoers Jesus came to redeem; the *stupid* evildoers He must refer back to the Creator and Preserver of the universe. "Father, forgive them; for they know not what they do."

Ah! those actions when we do not know—do not even try to know. May God be merciful, and may we determine that we will seek to understand! From knowledge to repentance, from repentance to the Cross, from the Cross to righteousness. Father, help us to know!

THE SECOND WORD

Verily I say unto thee, To day shalt thou be with me in paradise.—Luke 23: 43

AS we meditate on the Second Word, we see before us not one cross, but three.

On the first cross is a criminal. Heavyladen with guilt, he is paying its human penalty with his death. He looks toward the center cross, and offers a sneer.

On the third cross is a criminal. Heavyladen with guilt, he is paying its human penalty with his death. He looks toward the center cross—then answers the sneer.

First, he sees that all the three crucified are suffering together. "The same condemnation."

Second, he recognizes the guilt of his fellow criminal and himself. "We indeed justly."

Third, he recognizes the difference of the center cross. "This man hath done nothing amiss."

That was all. (1) I am in trouble. (2) The reason: I have sinned. (3) Is there a better way? Yes, that of the unsinning Person.

Trouble—repentance—faith. No wonder the second criminal burst forth, "Lord, remember me when thou comest into thy kingdom!"

And that leads us—as every agony of man must—to the center Cross. The Man on it was near death. But if He had been much closer to death than He was; if He had already said, "It is finished"; He yet would have called back to the criminal an answer—"Today shalt thou be with me in paradise."

We Christians see in the Cross the embodiment of redemption. Surely the incident of the Second Word is the kernel of the redemptive Cross—and the three crosses now divide for us into the one Cross and the two crosses.

For on the outside crosses hangs the world's need, which, like the poor, is always with us. Great sin and great suffering are there. Whichever is easier—to say, "Thy sins be forgiven thee," or to say, "Arise, and walk"—the two conditions include all of human evil as we know it.

And in the midst of the evil, sharing it, bearing it, hangs the world's Saviour, proclaiming eternally that all of the creation, preservation, and infinite resourcefulness of God is solemnly dedicated to the removal of the evil and the healing of its hurt.

Just to what extent this can always be accomplished is still obscure. Our Lord did not say, "You are now freed from all pain and suffering." Yet what He did say holds out the maximum hope of exactly that redemption in two remarkable ways.

In the first place, Jesus covered both the present life and the life after death. Whatever the theological difficulties involved in the statement of time in the Second Word, for the sinner and sufferer there is a grand promise: "I will help you *now,* and I will help you *forever: today* you shall be in *paradise."*

In this matter of when Jesus gives us His help the pendulum keeps swinging. Are we saved to live better, happier lives now? Are we saved to enjoy a blessed eternity? In the few words Jesus spoke to the criminal the latter was assured of both. For whatever hours of crucifixion remained the malefactor was strengthened and blessed. In the eternity which even then stared him in the face he was assured of triumph.

In the second place, Jesus offered Himself. "Thou shalt be with me," He said. "I too am on a cross, a fellow sufferer. Whatever the reasons why you are suffering and I am suffering, you can know that I am with you in the pain. As I expect sorrow to give way later on to joy, so you shall share my hope and its fulfillment . . ."

"You say someone has sprinkled pepper around?" It was

the commandant of a military school speaking. A calisthenic drill was being held in a closed room. A mischievous lad had discovered a way to create excitement. Boys were coughing and sneezing. A student officer reported that conditions were almost intolerable.

"I'll come and finish the drill with you," continued the commandant. As his military figure entered the room, and as he stayed throughout the unpleasant session, freshmen and sophomores were thrilled with their major's willingness to share their discomfort.

To the criminal, then, Jesus held out redemption utterly unbound by time, and utterly bound by His divine presence. From cross to Cross—"Help!" From Cross to cross—"I can and will!" A sorrow-cursed, sin-sick world can ask no more.

Yet there is always that first rejecting cross with its sneer, "Save thyself and us." Not everyone, it seems, can understand that true redemption involves not saving oneself. This renunciation should have been to the criminal the first evidence of Jesus' Saviourhood. Perhaps today the reason many do not recognize the center Cross is because they see salvation only in terms of mass selfishness. "Save thyself and us!"—but Jesus was busy trying to save a world.

THE THIRD WORD

Woman, behold thy son!—Behold thy mother!
—John 19: 26, 27

WHEN juvenile courts become discouraged with the conduct of youth; when educators feel that their influence is overthrown by what the child already is before they get him;

when the Church weighs the sources of its power; when, last of all, governments seek to stabilize, defend, or enlarge their countries—they all turn back to the place where man and woman, bound together in love, create and nourish the new members of the race—the home.

No wonder, then, that the Saviour on His cross fixed His gaze on His mother. He may have been thinking backward to His own life as a boy at home. He may have been thinking forward to the decisive influence the home would exert on all generations to come. He may have felt that in saving the world He would have to save the home, so that the home would help Him with the rest. In any case the Third Word is addressed, very personally, to home life. And Jesus by means of that word from the Cross, made three facts about home life clear.

The first is that, according to Jesus' way of life, the aged are an integral part of the family—as much as the young. The burden of the support of life necessarily rests on those in the prime of life. But these burden bearers have, not one, but two or three classes of persons to provide for: those not mature enough to provide for themselves—the children; those incapable of providing for themselves—the sick and handicapped; and those too far beyond life's normal strength to provide for themselves—the old people.

Jesus was not content to leave His earthly life without arranging for His mother's care. The arrangement He made was simple, complete, and effective. He did not consign Mary to a life of loneliness. He did not thrust her among total strangers—a disposition not to be thought of when any other is possible. He placed her with His nearest human friend.

One wonders whether Mary, the mother of at least eight children, had learned to be patient, forbearing, considerate—the kind of woman who could fit into a new living situation. Whether she had or not, Jesus did not raise the question. It was part of the life of a competent Carpenter—nailed now to a piece of furniture He never would have fashioned—to support the existence of His mother.

The second fact made clear by the Third Word is that blood relationship is only an incidental feature of the home. Obviously when natural ties are present, the family proceeds through them. But that they are unnecessary is illustrated on the Cross; for Mary and the beloved disciple may have been quite unrelated. And the Saviour here—as throughout Good Friday—is emphasizing what He taught before.

Remember the occasion when Jesus' mother and brothers stood without, wanting to see Him? But Jesus chose His family from the persons in the crowd. "Whosoever shall do the will of God, the same is my brother, and my sister, and mother." Jesus could find relatives anywhere!

Life's experience supports Jesus' contention. In how many homes an adopted child is welcomed and reared with mutual blessing! And there are numerous cases where several women, living together, make a fine home for children. It is a matter of consecration and concern, not of sex and blood. When circumstances require it, the creation of a home from artificial relationships is a fine art indeed—an art made use of on the Cross.

The third fact made clear is that Jesus was a man of warm-blooded soul rather than an imperturbable intellect. His biting indignation against the calloused Pharisees proves Jesus' warmth; so does this act of affection from the Cross!

On many counts Jesus is compared with the Athenian martyr, Socrates. In connection with the Third Word there comes to mind the story Plato tells of Socrates' death. The condemned Athenian's wife, Xanthippe, came to see him. Always a peevish, uncontrolled creature, Xanthippe was sobbing violently. "Take her away!" was the response of her blase husband; "if she stays here crying so hysterically, I may not be able to die with the calmness which befits a philosopher."

"Take her away!" The Son of God has many superiorities over the Greek Socrates, not least of which is Jesus' response to the woman nearest Him in human relationship, when she stood by the Cross mourning His untimely sacrifice. "Behold thy son!" He said to her—and thus sanctified the home not only in His birth, His childhood obedience, and His manhood support, but also in His death.

THE FOURTH WORD

My God, my God, why hast thou forsaken me?
—Matthew 27: 46

NOWHERE in all history is there a bitterer cry than this of Jesus from the Cross. He seems to have reached, when He uttered it, the deepest, most unfathomable waters of all the ocean of sin and grief and resultant Crucifixion. Jesus in His cry used the words of the Twenty-second Psalm. Like many another dying person, in His last utterances He either contented Himself with the simplest of affirmations, or repeated words from the past imbedded in His heart.

Again and again we ask ourselves why Jesus, the Son of God, reached a point of despair as terrible as that implied by this cry. The authenticity of the words is indisputable. Their implications cannot be side-stepped.

If we would at least partly understand the soul of the Master, we must think of Him as being engulfed with the burden of the world's misery and wrong, as well as with the dissolution of a physical body whose breath was almost gone. And for the moment, at least, the sustaining power of eternal hope was withdrawn. Jesus, appraising His work up to that point, was rendering Himself a verdict of complete failure.

I doubt whether the Saviour included in this verdict any great concern over His own human suffering—either the personal agony on the cross, or the injustice, the ignominy, and the persecutions of the preceding hours. Not only, in a spirit of sentimental coddling, do we commonly underestimate the physical bravery of Jesus; but He had clearly decided that suffering and sacrifice to the last drop were demanded of Him. But the question must have remained, Was the sacrifice worth while? For the moment, with the clouds sweeping over His soul, Jesus' answer was No.

The first of these clouds may have been the lack of appeal of the Cross itself. Jesus had predicted, "I, if I be lifted up from the earth, will draw all men unto me" (John 12: 32). But now he had been lifted up; and instead of all men seeing in His courage and crucifixion the certification of the Messiah and Redeemer, they were ridiculing Him or—still worse—ignoring Him.

Another cloud must have been the desertion of Jesus' loved

ones. Humanly speaking, nothing might have given Jesus more strength than if those closest to Him, sympathizing to the full with His divine enterprise, had said by their actions (instead of their words!), "Master, whatever befalls, we will assist Thee courageously until the end." Instead, Jesus had received from His own companions misunderstanding, misplaced bravado, and, in the end, actual abandonment. An exact parallel to the Fourth Word from the Cross are those other words of Matthew, "Then all the disciples forsook him, and fled."

A third cloud in the blanketing of God's sunlight must have been the total lack of comprehension, on the part of anyone, of what Jesus had been doing. Looking back, we see Jesus' work in the bright light of perspective as that of divine Teacher, Liver, Messiah, and Redeemer. Jesus' associates seem to have regarded Him variously as a sympathetic healer, a teller of attractive stories, a soothsayer, a wonder-worker, a messianic pretender, a social insurgent, or a political radical or reactionary: they were unable to equate what was constructive in these judgments with Jesus, the Only-begotten of God. At this point, with God's purpose and future eclipsed, there remained only these inadequate judgments of Jesus' fellows to torment Him. For it is significant that Jesus' inner feelings and hopes, even from a human point of view, are better represented by our perspective than by contemporary appraisal.

Then do we hear in this Fourth Word a cry that speaks failure to us? Nay, another factor enters the situation. Jesus acknowledged the removal of God; but He did not surrender the righteousness to which He had dedicated His existence!

Even though all token of God's later vindication was withheld, Jesus on the cross never weakened in His permanent conviction of what was right. This is for us the triumph in what for Jesus seemed failure.

Perhaps there was no other way than the way God took by which Jesus could have finally revealed His love of righteousness to us. Because God forsook Jesus, we can know that Jesus, with or without what are sometimes called "divine sanctions," is—yesterday, today, and forever—the incarnation of righteousness. As in every instance, we Christians now rejoice in an achievement which brought only pain to the Crucified One. Through utter despair He clung to the right.

THE FIFTH WORD

I thirst.—John 19: 28

A PERSON following the story of the Seven Words for the first time might begin to ask impatiently, "When does Jesus say something about Himself and His suffering?" We must wait until the Fifth Word before there is an answer to this question. Jesus first of all disposed of several situations surrounding the Crucifixion; next He turned to a consideration of the seeming failure of His efforts. Only then, with these problems laid aside, do we find that Jesus can think of Himself. The Fifth Saying is almost the simplest cry in the world of those who are fainting with weariness, agonized by suffering, parched unto death—"I thirst."

There is a simple corrective in the pure humanity of the Fifth Word of Jesus. There are those who, having made of sacrifice a fantasy of escape from the humdrum cares of the world, have demeaned and needlessly persecuted the body as an additional object of morbid renunciation. The Master, by this Word as by all His life, places a practical stamp on sacrifice. When you are serving others by what you do, there is no limit to the degree of sacrifice which is admirable, even to the point of suffering and death. But when you are not serving a constructive purpose, self-infliction of suffering is not part of the Kingdom of God. Christ's rule is simple: When it hurts no one, be happy; when it helps someone, suffer.

Thus, at last, Jesus came to think of Himself. One simple need He had which others could gratify for Him. Always as willing to receive from others as He was eager to share with others, Jesus let it be known that His frame was racked with thirst.

Amidst all the callousness and harshness of the judges, mob, and soldiers, we seem to witness here a genuine act of kindness toward Jesus. The liquid given Him was probably a preparation intended to relieve thirst and pain. John tells us that Jesus "received" it. It was as if God, compelled for His own eternal reasons to withdraw Himself from Jesus up above, could not resist coming back to His Only-begotten through the milk of human kindness—a milk which always has been and—please Him—always will be a part of God's creation and natural revelation.

To this day, listening to authentic stories of the treatment of prisoners of war by captors taught to hate them (with full subtraction of the powerful undertow of war propaganda and sensational storymaking), one is yet amazed at the acts of simple helpfulness which can go on among sworn enemies. Human instinct, when uncontrolled by instilled malice, tends toward the slaking of even an enemy's thirst!

In this Word, then, Jesus refers to Himself. If we are still surprised that He thought of Himself at all, we may profit by comparing His order of preference with ours. The average human being usually thinks first of himself; second, of his family; third, of those who do wrong; last of all, of his enemies. According to the Words from the Cross, Jesus thought first of His enemies; second, of those who do wrong; third, of His family; and last of all, of Himself.

In Jesus' lifetime, when He was strong, He also thirsted. Then, we are told, He used His thirst as the means of rescuing the character of a Samaritan woman of careless life; nor are we informed that His physical thirst was quenched. It was only when Jesus was weakened with suffering that He was willing to accept relief. When Jesus was strong, He disdained to know the sheltered luxury of the foxes, which had holes, and of the birds, which had nests. It was only when others got hold of Him that He was willing to accept the shelter of the bed of the Cross. The Fifth Cry from the Cross may be called the exception which proves the rule of Jesus' selflessness.

THE SIXTH WORD

It is finished—John 19: 30

WITH the last two Words from the Cross we leave the Jesus of pain and dejection to hear the cries which concluded His human life. The Seventh Word anticipates the future. This Word—"It is finished"—is Jesus' verdict upon the past.

Let us ask ourselves what, for Jesus, was finished. Beginning at the inmost circle, there was, first of all, the Crucifixion itself. Those hours were coming to a close. Then there were the struggle and suffering of Holy Week. The last week of Lent was near its end. In the next circumference was Jesus' purposeful ministry—His definite decision to do what God had planned for man's redemption. This was terminating. Beyond that, Jesus' whole life of unsullied integrity was drawing to a close. And in the still larger orbit the spiritual hopes of centuries of Judaism were culminating. Much, indeed, was finished!

But it is almost impossible for us to enter into the full significance of the Sixth Word unless we examine this Saying in its commonest meaning in the language in which it comes to us. There is only one word in Greek for the three English words, "It is finished"—*tetelestai.* When work is finished in the sense of *tetelestai,* it does not mean that a whistle blows, the workman drops his tools, and in the middle of a job leaves for lunch! It means that the piece of work or task is completed, made perfect, and there is nothing more to be done on it. From this Greek word are derived the technical terms which signify the utmost conception of "purpose" as determining the universe.

When Jesus spoke the sixth time from the Cross, therefore, He was not saying that because of the waning of His physical strength He would have to stop; but rather that the various circles of His endeavor had been completed and brought to perfect form. Virtually Jesus was saying at this very last opportunity what He had said before: "I have finished the work which thou gavest me to do."

From the creation onward God had been planning for the children of men those physical and social and spiritual gifts which could mean redemption and happiness for them. In God's great plan Jesus found Himself having a central and decisive place. If He properly filled that place, God's plan and all God's purposes were fulfilled. If Jesus did not accomplish what God expected of Him, God's plan and purposes—even if not annulled—would be distorted. In the Sixth Word Jesus proclaims that in His judgment He has completed His assignment and has done it as well as God expected Him to do it. The Servant of the Lord, on His Cross, was seeing of the travail of His soul, and was being satisfied. His task had been perfectly accomplished.

Two other considerations grow out of this confidence of Jesus on the cross. The first is this: Christian thought ever since has so fully accepted and substantiated Jesus' claim, that in all our theology the Death on the Cross is accepted as the perfect conclusion of God's work of atonement and of all that Jesus came on earth to do. The rest—the days in the grave, the Resurrection, the Ascension—are a matter of vindication and triumph. But the assignment of the task was completed exactly when Jesus said, "It is finished."

The other consideration is one for us personally. As the eternal Father made Jesus the center of His great purpose and plan, so He also wishes to make each one of us the center of some plan and purpose of His—however fractional or humble. We therefore in all of our living have an obligation to God to strive for the same perfection of workmanship as Jesus attained.

A carpenter once told me that he believed that Jesus, when He worked in the carpenter shop of Nazareth, must have been the kind of craftsman who did whatever He did accurately and perfectly. If He made a table, the table would stand four-square and firm. Jesus, as the worker of perfection in divine things, suggested to the present-day carpenter Jesus, the worker of perfection in human activities.

Some said *of* Jesus, "He hath done all things well." Let us at least aim to say *with* Jesus, "It is finished: I have finished the work which thou gavest me to do."

THE SEVENTH WORD

Father, into thy hands I commend my spirit.
—Luke 23: 46

AS a traveler, wearied by a slow, dark, hot, smoky passage through a long tunnel, rejoices when his train bursts forth into the light; as an insomniac, wearied with the unending hours of a sleepless night, rejoices at the first hints of dawn: so the worshiper, waiting at the Cross of Christ, rejoices at the light of the triumphant Seventh Word.

Our Lord endured all the doubt and frustration of anyone whose death is hard; but His last utterance was for Him a word of complete trust in God, for us a word of complete satisfaction that all is well for the world. When our Saviour was in His deepest distress He quoted a sentence from the Psalms. Now in His moment of release and contentment He again takes hold of the Psalms, quoting from the Thirty-first Psalm words which the Revised Version translates, "Into thy hand I commend my spirit."

But now Jesus adds a word which is nowhere in the Psalm —the word "Father." This is a special sign that the light of God's love was clearly revealed to Jesus again. Once more the Master is dealing with the same God in the consciousness of whose Fatherhood He had gone forth among the ways of men to redeem the world. The Father who had sent Him forth, the Father who had been with Him in His ministry, the Father who had led Him to the cross, is still the Father into whose house of many mansions He Himself is returning, and into whose hands with unquestioning trust He commends His spirit.

In all this latter rhythm of the Cross there is a necessary lesson for us, as we struggle through pain, disappointment, disillusion, and personal disaster of any kind. In human predicaments there usually comes a time when God's face cannot be found. The Christian is tempted to cry out in his despair, "Why hast thou forsaken me?" In the worst cases repeated prayer, and the apparent surrender to God of one's whole life on a cross of pain, produce no results.

To any who thus share the darkness of the Saviour's Fourth Word, the message of the Seventh Word—or perhaps of the last two words—is life-giving food. If the Christian maintains his integrity, and continues to seek God, eventually the Father in all His mercy will be revealed again as possessing the love that passeth understanding.

And here the Sixth Word offers a helpful prerequisite. Are we sure—in our tortured pain—that we have taken the place which God has assigned us as well as we are able? Perhaps by our pain and our frustration God's will is being accomplished in some way which we have not been willing to recognize. It was only after Jesus could feel and say that his God-given task had been fulfilled that He was once more able to say, "Father."

The Seventh Word binds the Crucifixion to everything that comes after it in Christian faith and history. One now begins to foresee dimly the vindication by the Almighty Power of the universe of Jesus and His work. Before yielding up His breath Jesus envisioned His career as part of God's eternal plan. Having carried out the part assigned Him, the Master commended to the handling of God the future of all His redemptive ministry and death. The Saviour in His last moments knew what the disciples later preached—that God would raise Him up, "having loosed the pains of death, because it was not possible that he should be holden of it." Jesus knew that His work would be continued—under God's own direction.

Jesus was right—even for this earth. No sooner had He given up the ghost than the officer in command of the crucifixion squad bore witness openly and emphatically that the Crucified One was a righteous man, the Son of God. The Resurrection—with its triumph, its divine vindication, and its implications of world-wide mission—was already on its way. Thus may we, seeking in the sorrow of Good Friday the fellowship of Christ's sufferings, look forward toward the brightness of Easter Day—when the Saviour comes forth with His Resurrection body; when the old leaven gives way to the unleavened bread of sincerity and truth; when the Cross of death and sacrifice becomes the Glory of mankind.

The Day of a Tomb in a Garden

Stuart Winfield Herman

SATURDAY IN HOLY WEEK

AND after this Joseph of Arimathæa, being a disciple of Jesus, but secretly for fear of the Jews, besought Pilate that he might take away the body of Jesus: and Pilate gave him leave. He came therefore, and took the body of Jesus.

And there came also Nicodemus, which at the first came to Jesus by night, and brought a mixture of myrrh and aloes, about an hundred pound weight.

Then took they the body of Jesus, and wound it in linen clothes with the spices, as the manner of the Jews is to bury.

Now in the place where he was crucified there was a garden; and in the garden a new sepulchre, wherein was never man yet laid. There laid they Jesus therefore because of the Jews' preparation day; for the sepulchre was nigh at hand.

—John 19: 38-42

The Day of a Tomb in a Garden

THE average earthly life is measured by thousands of days, not one of which is an exact duplicate of another. As each leaf on a tree differs from the others so is it with the days of each life. There are high and low, full and empty, joyous and sad days. Some of these days leave their marks upon the body, mind or soul in a manner which nothing can erase. Were we asked to name the days, which have left the greatest impress and have contributed the most marked influence upon our life, it would be comparatively easy to do. Not a single day is without peculiar significance in each life, although it may not be recognized as such. However, every life has its great days without which the life would be largely unintelligible.

We are concerned in this study with the days in the earthly life of Our Lord Jesus. In the economy of God no doubt each day was planned as a necessary part of the perfect whole. We cannot think of His life with the subtraction of a single moment from the cradle to the tomb. Seeing that we have come in our studies to the Day of the Tomb in the Garden, it might be profitable to recall the Days of Crisis from the beginning of His earthly career until its tragic close. Time and space cannot permit the recording of the days upon which He spake His revealing words, accomplished His miraculous deeds, and underwent the climacteric incidents of His career. Never was an earthly life lived which was crowded with such majesty and glory, yet so concealed by humility and sacrificial service.

The last week contained days full to overflowing of words and deeds which have become a treasure house of inestimable blessing for all mankind. The Palm Sunday acclaim and reception despite its deep undertones; the visits to and the talks in the Temple with their illuminating incidents and lessons; the fellowship and ministry with disciples and other loved ones; the unforgettable gathering in the Upper Room for the institution and administration of the Holy Supper and the utterance of prayer; the betrayals and denials, so shockingly modern and personal; the Good Friday, with the never-dying words of the ever-living Word, constitute a galaxy of days such as the world has never known. And, then, at the end of this greatest of weeks came the day of the interment of His Body in the tomb in a garden. So, at the close of this most tragical of days since the creation of the world, secret disciples, for fear of the Jews, request His Body from the cowardly ruler, and after embalming it in costly spices, place it in a new tomb. What a seemingly sad ending to the story of the most perfect and beautiful life ever lived. The dead body in the sealed tomb seems so hopelessly final for the hoped for Redeemer of the World. There is not a shred of hope in any heart now that the blackest deed has taken place and the Roman guard has been placed so that His fearful followers cannot rob the tomb of His lifeless body. If Good Friday was a day of heartbreak and crushing despair, how utterly dark also must have been the Saturday that followed.

It might be well for those of us who are His followers, close or far off, to review somewhat the thoughts of those who had a part so long ago in the dark, dark day in a garden in which there was a new tomb.

To Pilate it must have been a day of deep uncertainty because he knew that he, in most cowardly fashion to save himself and his unsavory administration, had given over an innocent victim to a shameful death. Henceforth his conscience would hound him and his hands would bear the stain of blood. One never stands in Lucerne and looks up at Mt. Pilatus, but that the tradition recurs of Pilate's incurable physical and mental disease and his suicide on that towering Alpine peak. Yes, that Saturday could have brought at its best a deep uncertainty to Pilate and perchance the beginnings of a remorse that ended even as tradition describes.

To the Roman Soldiers—who were obedient to their officers it must have seemed that they had complied with a disgraceful duty. The garments for which they had cast dice were of comparatively little value. The fearsome phenomena of earthquake, storm, and open tombs were mysteries too profound for them and could not be accounted for by their experience with their superstitions. It was not for them to question this dark deed. However, there must have been a feeling of security in that they knew the tomb of this strange man was sealed over which they were set as guards. The sooner this task was over the better they would feel.

To the Roman Centurion—there would continue to sound in his very soul those unparalleled words which he heard from that central cross. He had witnessed many violent deaths, but never one like this; he had heard many last words, but none with such divine content and emphasis as these. Over and over there would be echoed in his heart his own confession, "Truly this was a Son of God." Somehow he must have wished he could have known such a matchless soldier of God far better, and possibly could have wished he might have been privileged to be one of His followers. He at least has made a good confession, which he would never retract.

To the Priests and to all the Jews—who had a part in His death that Saturday must have been a day of mingled emotions. Some who thought that death settles things felt boastfully confident that this blasphemer and troublemaker was forever silenced; some who recalled his dying and were made fearful by the unearthly portents that followed were rather disturbed as they reviewed their part which they had undertaken at the instigation of their leaders, and some must have begun to feel a sense of remorse as they recalled the kind words He had spoken, the helpful works He was reported to have done, and His deep sympathy for all to whom he had ministered. No doubt that sealed tomb contained the body of a young man, who was not deserving of such a death and might have done even greater things had he not been crucified. But they were as helpless to do anything about it as are peoples in great nations today who are held in practical bondage by criminally wicked leaders. More to be pitied is this later group than to be bitterly censured.

To the Disciples—that Saturday must have been a day of unmeasured self-censure, repentance, and heartbreak. They had "followed afar off" when He needed their heartwhole loyalty.

Whether by betrayal, denial or fear for self they had discounted their promised allegiance and had failed in their friendship, when friendship would have covered a multitude of lesser defects. Their hopes for self, for loved ones, for their nation were shattered. Soon they also might be spectacles for a curious, mocking rabble on other crosses. Now they see that desertion of a great leader or of a great idea is not worth the questionable safety promised. If, if only they had not "followed afar off." Yet, out of their deep distress and by reason of their sincere repentance, there may have come, through the grace of God, a glimmer of hope that somehow such goodness, as was His and exercised in their behalf, could not be expended in vain, that in and through His infinite resources there would be given them strength and courage to carry on, even if not in the fullness of their great hopes for the establishment of His Kingdom. One thing they must do—they must be true to each other, they must comply with His great prayer in the Upper Room. They must be one and one in God. But the blackness of that day in which they groped so hopelessly, when the foundations of hope seemed utterly above their utmost reach, could never be forgotten.

To the Women and John—the day brought the sorrow that comes to such as love without a trace of selfishness, who love because of the qualities of goodness and loving kindness which they had seen in daily association and had come to love. In blind love, which surrendered every doubt to His will they loved on and determined to continue to love and to minister as best they could. To them, if death had really come to Him, they had known love and life at their best and tomorrow morning early they would be at the tomb to demonstrate their undying, unchanging loyalty and love. Their love could stand whatever strain of fear and doubt, dismay and lack of complete understanding that could be put upon it. The spark of hope could not be totally extinguished in their hearts, although they may have thought the "black out" of hope was total.

To Joseph and to Nicodemus, who came at long last to evidence a faith which had grown by reason of testimony from the lips of Jesus and from others, who out of prejudice and fear of others dared to claim a body that must defile and to undertake a costly task that must ostracize from former associates and loved ones. Their day was a day of profound regret at having at length found courage to minister to one so despised and lonely, and, at the same time, a satisfaction that courage had been given them to do this last sad ministry of faith in Him who was so lonely. Theirs to share a tomb and to fill the world with the aroma of the spices.

To the Lord Jesus—the Victory had been won. What He had come to do had been accomplished. Into His Father's hand He had commended His Spirit and all was well. His ministry to departed spirits was being accomplished. He looked forward with joy to the coming morning when He would fulfill His Word that He would rise again. With Him all is certainty and victory! To Him it must have been a day of great spiritual refreshment and holy communion.

To us—it ought to bring measureless peace and confidence. He truly died and conquered death for us. When our trust is in Him we need fear no evil for all will be well with our soul. The world, the flesh and the devil may strive to do us harm, but they can have no power over us when our ally is the Triune God,—Father, Son and Holy Ghost. Death and its terrors are conquered and we are more than conquerors through Christ Jesus, who loved us, gave Himself for us, and loves us still with everlasting love.

It was a blessed day for us—that day in a tomb in a garden.

"Who is this that comes in glory
With the trump of jubilee?
Lord of battles, God of armies,
He has gained the victory!
He who on the Cross did suffer,
He who from the grave arose,
He has vanquished sin and Satan,
He by death has spoiled His foes."

EASTER DAY

But Christ Did Rise!

Paul Scherer

EASTER DAY

IN the end of the sabbath, as it began to dawn toward the first day of the week, came Mary Magdalene, and the other Mary, to see the sepulchre. And, behold, there was a great earthquake: for the angel of the Lord descended from heaven, and came and rolled back the stone from the door, and sat upon it. His countenance was like lightning, and his raiment white as snow: and for fear of him the keepers did shake, and became as dead men.

And the angel answered and said unto the women, "Fear not ye: for I know that ye seek Jesus, which was crucified. He is not here; for he is risen, as he said. Come, see the place where the Lord lay. And go quickly, and tell his disciples that he is risen from the dead; and, behold, he goeth before you into Galilee; there shall ye see him: lo, I have told you."

And they departed quickly from the sepulchre, with fear and great joy, and did run to bring his disciples word.

And as they went to tell his disciples, behold, Jesus met them, saying, "All hail." And they came and held him by the feet, and worshipped him.

Then said Jesus unto them, "Be not afraid: go tell my brethren, that they go into Galilee, and there shall they see me."

—*Matthew 28: 1-10*

But Christ Did Rise!

Thou, O Lord, who wast dead and art alive forevermore, who standest now in our midst, we adore Thee; and beseech Thee that from whatever condition we come Thou wouldst lead us beyond it toward Thy purpose. Amen.

FROM that time forth we begin to see in perspective what a difference the resurrection made: how it gave a new and deeper significance to the very fact of being alive in the world. There was never much attempt at the first to prove what had happened. It wasn't necessary. Anybody who wanted to could collect the evidence for himself. He had been seen, this Jesus, by over five hundred people at once. So writes Paul. You could go and ask them. They were still living, most of them.

The New Testament at least bothers with it no further. If it had been a fiction, every hour wide open to rebuttal, it could hardly have held up in a world fiercer even than ours a little crowd of men and women that had scrambled to their feet on the basis of something they had seen and overthrew an Empire. The New Testament bothers only with Jesus, and how that first Easter changed the whole front of human existence. The essential thing about it wasn't an argument. The essential thing about food isn't either! The essential thing about it was the difference it made, and always will! That's what I want you to look at now. And I want you to go back to the very day it happened.

The disciples were in the same kind of dilemma we're in: they loved the past, they didn't believe in the present, and they dreaded the future. That was the situation; when suddenly they came face to face with the only thing on earth that could ever have transformed it. No matter what the facts were now, this *Jesus* was still a fact too; and other facts had a way of running into Him! It hadn't been *easy* to believe in the Carpenter from Nazareth. The Sanhedrin, which was the Board of Trustees and Executive Committee of the Church of God in Palestine, wouldn't have anything to do with Him. All the self-acclaimed patriots despised Him. And they had made Him eat His words. He had died out there on that hill just as any man would have died. It wasn't easy. These were the facts, and you had to hold with the facts!

Until they collided with a God who paid no attention to them! Except to thaw them out and set them on the go, as the sun breaks the cold, iron grip of winter. He got them all mixed up with hope again; marched His friends out with blood and tears, with clenched hands; turned everybody that loved Him right about face. I wonder sometimes why Easter didn't rob living of *all* its significance. It transcended their world so far, you might think it would have left history and all their busy goings on without any shred of meaning. Why should anybody fool with anything any longer? With such grandeur in your soul as this gives you, you could afford to look down on the whole business and make nothing of it!

It just didn't work that way, that's all: for a little while, yes; but soon it threw them into things. They got in deeper than they had ever been. They got in to shape and mould and lift what they touched. They got in to make the days fit better into what they had learned about this world of God. Immortality wasn't just a state of being which would follow death, may be: there were ways of being immortal now; the other kind didn't matter much. Down at the center of it all, where men were at their busiest, *these* men began to match their step with Christ's; and He always had lived His immortality!

This is what they saw when they looked back. You couldn't shove Jesus and God around on Calvary and be rid of them. You couldn't finish off the Sermon on the Mount with a grin and a hammer! *The Christian Century* says it's abrogated for the duration. People said, No, to it once before, and God said, Yes. You couldn't bring *any* of it to a deadletter office. Life was intent on something else besides just dying off at the top. It wasn't only moving, it was going somewhere; and nails couldn't stop it, and a grave couldn't stop it. God had vindicated every word He had ever said, and redeemed His pledge! Pilate and Caiaphas and that Good Friday crowd had tried to draw a line through the gospels and cancel them; "Blessed are the meek for they shall inherit the earth. . . ." And there they crucified Him. But the Author of all things had written across the original text in His own hand, *Stet!* Let it stand! Let it stand forever!

That's what had pushed out the horizons! And it would again if you wouldn't keep holding back. Do you remember how it was four hundred years ago? How many voyagers set sail for rumoured lands! Columbus among them. Braved distant winds and unknown shores. And how they came back with queer tales and fabled wealth; and nobody could get over it. The Renaissance broke, and the Reformation, flooding the stagnant life of Europe. Poetry, romance. And the world was young again!

It's what would happen now if you'd let this glory really get its grip on you. It wasn't for the disciples; it isn't for us, to be throwing ourselves away, grunting and gobbling round the trough, as someone has put it, shoving and pushing for what we can get; cringing in front of some anxiety; cowed by some petty sin; driven, beaten down, always condemned to be this! The New Testament keeps looking from you to the Resurrection-story, and back again: amazed to find you crouching behind any chance shelter you can dig up; being so prudent and judicious and safe. You weren't intended for these puny quarters where so many of us by choice live our dull lives. You were made for the wide and dangerous edge of things.

"Hide me, O my Saviour, hide,
Till the storm of life is past,
Safe into the haven guide,
O receive my soul at last."

It's all right for people who haven't much view; it isn't for us, who have our feet set this day in a large place, with the winds of Eternity blowing!

For God's sake and your own, for the sake of these coming years which we shall have to live through whether we like them or not, don't allow this splendour to die out of the human soul for any slovenliness of yours! I can't tell how much time we have left to get back to it. I said that four years ago this Easter. I said, I was terrified of a future without God, without any faith in the dignity of human life, without any horizons at all. I said, it wasn't funny facing that; and it hasn't been! The last sight Jesus had of His disciples, they were running away. This may be the last sight He'll have of some of us for a long time to come. And they were wretched without Him. So are we, if we'd be honest with ourselves!

Look! We have come here very much as these disciples were: in love with the past, without much belief in the present, and dreading the future. All of us have seen better times. If only the times to come could be as those times! When we were making money hand over fist, and didn't have to lay it all out for arms and ammunition. When meat and butter were plentiful, and our boys were at home, and we could go and come in our cars as we pleased. The world as we knew it fifteen years ago, with everybody looking out for himself and forging ahead. When we actually get down to a peace-table, that's what we want back. We'd like very much, if you don't mind, to reestablish the *status quo ante;* it was a good old status!

In the light of this risen Christ, I say to you it's gone, irrevocably gone. You'll never lay eyes on it any more. Go! Tell His disciples and Peter that He goeth before you into Galilee. There shall ye see Him! The past is full of dry-rot, no matter how much you've loved it or hated it! I've been around through my share of it, and my share of it has been delightful. But this Christ I want more than anything else to follow isn't bound by it. You don't plough a furrow by looking over your shoulder: you turn into a pillar of salt, with Lot's wife! Life is a serial story. The real glory of it lies in the words, "To be continued." That's the whole gospel. Gird yourself for it!

He is not here: He is risen. Before His living face we've got to quit believing in the past and believe in the present. For these disciples, darkness had wrapped itself like a mantle around everything. And then suddenly the light broke through, and everywhere it was morning! How often do you think that's happened in human life? Just when the dark is deepest, it's dawn. It's a proverb, isn't it? And a proverb is something which generations have found so true that they have had to put it up in amber, press it into a mould to keep it.

But what I'd sooner see you get hold of is the fact behind it. Back of all these constant changes for the better is always somebody's stubborn belief in the present; somebody's courageous use of every average, passing day. That could be proved from history. Somebody believed in the transcontinental railroad while Webster was fighting it in Congress. Somebody believed in the airplane while the public was trying to laugh it out of court. I wish Matthew, Peter, James, John, Andrew, Bartholomew had done a little believing in something the night they locked themselves in a room. They were like a child shut up indoors on a rainy day, not caring for its toys; pressing its nose against the glass; looking out on a dismal world. They thought it was the end, and it was the beginning! There had been a promise, and they had forgotten it: but Jesus hadn't. When all at once it came alive in front of their very eyes! "Peace be unto you!" He hadn't quit. And God hadn't quit. It wasn't just the past that was holy ground: it was the present! They'd better unlock the door and get into it! And they did!

Down in Washington there's a marble building where the Government keeps the archives of the United States. On one stoop is carved the inscription, "What is Past is Prologue." And it isn't so! The past precedes, but it doesn't determine what is to be. The real prologue to the future is the present. Let them carve that in marble down in Washington! That gives you to think! What we are doing at this moment isn't a simple handing on of the pressures which are back there in our history: we're actively shaping today the things to come! Why on earth do we keep suggesting to ourselves, that what now is doesn't matter much?—poor stuff,—routine. It used to be better. It may be better again. But it's bad enough at this writing. Something to live *through!* And it's the only creative moment there is! That's where you bend things right, or let them veer off into something worse. When you're cheated, it isn't hope that cheats you. It isn't life that cheats you. That's nonsense. It's the *Now* cheating the after-a-while!

May be this is our chance, as it was theirs! It called for every talent they had. It's calling for ours. We've dreamed about a new heaven and a new earth, just as they had; and thought that perhaps it would come without us. It won't—ever! We wonder why life is as it is. We've been so patient, and nothing has come of it. The CIO goes on strike again. Germany and Japan want to take over the world. The fellow who hurt my feelings last week hurts them again this week, and in exactly the same place! Nothing will ever come of any of it until we stop trying to put up with all of it and start handling at least some of it! Rumors get going. What do you do? Give them a little fillip with your tongue? Misunderstandings break loose. You see the rift growing wider. Isn't it too bad? And you leave it where it was! It's the *Now* cheating the after-a-while.

And it will cheat us of the peace we want among the nations if we start backing out of this world again, even before the war's over! It will cheat us of our faith, lock, stock, and barrel, if we don't fling in the world's face a few convictions today that won't shake day-after-tomorrow! It isn't the past that does us in, it's the present! God help us if we play about with *any* of it any longer! Or let anything that's wrong *stay* wrong for lack of us!

But what about the future? Well, you don't have to face it by yourself. God's plan wasn't finished. It wasn't beaten when they drove those nails into that wood. The "farce" of Jesus of Nazareth wasn't played out! "He is not here: he is risen!" You can face the *future* with that—if you want to. They did, and whipped it to a standstill! Not with any make-believe religion that they took off and put on whenever they felt like it! They whipped it with their faith in a Man who wouldn't stay dead, a Man who went stalking through death like somebody blazing a trail through undiscovered country, carrying the frontiers with Him, heading straight for the lands beyond the sunset, and bringing back the title-deeds in His pocket! They threw in on that everything they had and what they were. The years ahead of them looked like a flood. It would creep up from knee to waist to chin. And God said, "March!" Just as He had said to the children of Israel that night they had run away from Egypt, with Pharaoh's host behind them and the waters of the Red Sea in front. Don't bother your head with what you think is yonder. I'm God here, and I'm God there, and I'm God over on the other side of it. Let's move! And the waters stood back, a wall on their right hand and on their left; and He made the sea dry land!

Call it romancing if you like. But you'll find it's true! Life is always simpler than we make it out to be. The only thing that complicates it is the way we go on saying No to God! When we change our tune, He'll change His response. And the miracle of His deliverance will come face on to meet us! Some day we'll look back on these years with a good deal of hindsight, and wonder why on earth we understood so little. This God is living, and not dead. And He wants us and means to have us,—or else! He has jockeyed us unto it now! We've got to decide!

At the Temple in Jerusalem, long years before Christ, the vast crowd used to wait, as James Stewart reminds us, eager and restless, for the moment to come when it would pledge itself again in renewed faith and obedience to Jehovah. At the appointed hour a priest carried forward a torch and set off the fire on the altar. As the flames leaped up, the stillness was shattered with a blast of music. Peal on peal it rang through the courts. And the old chronicler set it down: when the burnt-offering began, the song of the Lord began also, with the trumpets! It's what the Devil said once he missed most in heaven: the sound of the trumpets in the morning! Can't we sound them any more?